DATE DUE

~~DE 20 98~~			
~~NO 1 01~~			
~~NO 20/01~~ ~~SE 19 01~~			

Government Is Good

Government Is Good

CITIZENSHIP,
PARTICIPATION,
AND POWER

—————
•

Joseph F. Freeman

University of Missouri Press

Columbia and London

5   4   3   2   1   96   95   94   93   92

Library of Congress Cataloging-in-Publication Data

Freeman, Joseph F., 1939–
    Government is good : citizenship, participation, and power /
Joseph F. Freeman.
        p.   cm.
    Includes bibliographical references.
    ISBN 0–8262–0821–5 (alk. paper) — ISBN 0–08262–0842–8 (pbk.)
    1. Political participation.   2. Politics, Practical.
3. Citizenship.   4. Power (Social sciences)   I. Title.
JF2051.F74   1992
323'.042—dc20   91–41744
                                                                       CIP

∞™ This paper meets the requirements of the
American National Standard for Permanence of Paper
for Printed Library Materials, Z39.48, 1984.

Designer: Elizabeth Fett
Typesetter: Connell-Zeko Type & Graphics
Printer and Binder: Thomson-Shore, Inc.
Typeface: Bem

IN MEMORIAM

L. M. S.
1887–1984

"If you want to write,
first you have to do something to write about."

Contents

Acknowledgments

Writing any manuscript is arduous, but this particular one required the additional effort of balancing the twin demands of academic life and active politics. I am truly grateful to all the people who helped in many ways to make doing both possible.

At the College, Jack remained the "generative spirit" who provided continued intellectual support for the heart of the project as well as coaching on the manuscript. Dan proved to be the best chairman I ever had and was a sympathetic and helpful reader. The Faculty Research Committee was always ready to grant my requests for support from its limited funds.

Since life at a small college can feel confined at times, friends and colleagues at other institutions were especially important. Al provided fuel for thought at critical times as well as intellectual guidance. At Tech, Charles read the manuscript and offered encouragement when I needed it. At the University, Dolph and the staff at the Institute provided resources and support at the beginning. Later on, at various times and in different ways, Clifton, Matt, and Tim provided important responses to help guide me. Thanks are also due Garrett and Carey for encouragement in the early phases.

The voters of Hill City, whose support made my political career possible, deserve thanks; I hope their trust was at least partially repaid by good service. Those who provided political support constitute a long list; I deeply appreciate them, especially Carroll. The staff members in City Hall have been professional and public-spirited; they serve Hill City well.

The friends who provided personal support while I did more than I had planned to must be mentioned: the Lob Five, especially Ed, who spins off juicy quotes and good thinking; various members of the Community Club, including Bill, who provided cheap, isolated quarters for the bulk of the writing, and Wayne, for good conversation at the right times; Christoph in Germany helped keep things in perspective at a couple of critical points; and Marvelous Marvin reappeared from my past to provide help and guidance in the home stretch.

Other friends to both me and Hill City that deserve mention include Jim, who encouraged the initial effort, provided professional advice, and probably thought the enterprise would never get finished. Sonny and Reggie helped materially; Louis and Charlotte did, too. In my office at the College, I was blessed at crucial times by staff that took more initiative than the job description mentioned and helped keep things in balance. Nina proved a superlative office manager and a valued friend when things were less than easy. Pansy and Kim (a.k.a. Moonbeam) helped keep the juggling act going.

Dawn put the manuscript together on a single disk, from an embarrassing number of fragments. Virginia deserves a special award for typing, troubleshooting, and correcting my word processing blunders, not to mention just putting up with my continual pestering.

Bev Jarrett and her staff at the University of Missouri Press are due a large measure of sheer gratitude, and the anonymous readers of the manuscript made substantial suggestions that helped make it much better than it would otherwise have been. Tim Fox did a superlative job of editing my messy prose.

Finally, I would like to give more thanks than can be fully expressed in words to my wife, Margie, and my sons, Jeff and Bill, for their patience, good humor, and support.

Government Is Good

[The townsman] takes a part in every occurrence in the place; he practices the art of government in the small sphere within his reach; he accustoms himself to those forms without which liberty can only advance by revolutions; he imbibes their spirit; he acquires a taste for order, comprehends the balance of powers, and collects clear practical notions on the nature of his duties and the extent of his rights. . . .

I believe that provincial institutions are useful to all nations, but nowhere do they appear to me to be more necessary than among a democratic people. . . . How can a populace unaccustomed to freedom in small concerns learn to use it temperately in great affairs? What resistance can be offered to tyranny in a country where each individual is weak and where the citizens are not united by any common interest?

—Alexis de Tocqueville, *Democracy in America*

Prologue

You know I hate, detest, and can't bear a lie, not because I am straighter
than the rest, but simply because it appalls me. There is a taint of death,
a flavor of mortality in lies. . . . It makes me miserable and sick,
like biting into something rotten would do.

—Joseph Conrad, *The Heart of Darkness*

There's no wind at all, but the dark, greasy water is moving anyway. Faint
eddies swirl around the pilings of the docks. A slight upward push on the
hulls of the weekend sailors' boats rocks them, making their rigging clatter
and their ropes creak. It seems like the harbor has too much water in it, its
surface swelling up toward the hazy sky. Are the low places in the fill dirt
around the dock staying wetter longer? Maybe the tide didn't go all the
way out at the last turn? There's no one to ask; no one around, no animate
presence at all, except for the flock of gulls screaming in anticipation of
more garbage. Out along the channel to the ocean even the familiar low
islands have changed—more black than green now, no longer displays of
earthly fertility, but something else, something sullen and secretly rebellious.

But surely this must be nonsense, my imagination playing tricks on
me—just fragments of nightmares caught up in a web of too little sleep,
too much to drink, and too much damnable late summer heat. Still, the
strange sense lingers that deep down something has shifted, some elemental balance has been undone forever, and the just-beginning accumulation
of millions of tiny breaks and displacements will eventually dissolve the
ground under our feet, leaving us to drown.

We like to imagine that great changes are brought on by sudden catastro-
phes, that storms are the most powerful things that the sea can press upon
us. A storm can, indeed, move sand, uproot trees, leave siding and shingles
on the ground. Yet the isolated and dramatic strength of a storm is nothing
compared to what would be done by just a small change in the relation of
the land and the ocean. (Funny how we would rather talk about the separate
components, analyzing them down to the tiniest imaginable detail, rather

than confront relationships and connections between the parts we analyze so diligently.) Just think what would happen if the ocean were to rise ten feet, or fifty, or a hundred. What a demonstration of power that would be!

The very start might not be conspicuous—the penetration of fresh groundwater by brackish seawater, the silent push of the sea up the broad tidal creeks, the uncounted capillary fingers of saltwater probing through sand and mud. But as it continued to seek its new level, the change would appear unmistakably, wiping out leisure-time yacht basins and fishermen's docks alike, finally oozing up into the littered, smog-wrapped cities.

Dare anyone ask if all these—the broad sand beaches, the ocean, the bays and inlets, the fish, the shellfish, and the birds—are things that are irrevocably here, for no other reason than that we want them to be? And how about the man-made things—the launching ramps, the dredged and marked channels, the rescue teams that will spare no expense to come to our aid when we run into a stump with the motor wide open? Not likely that anyone will ask. It seems to be fashionable to believe that the universe is centered on oneself and, accordingly, if you concentrate on yourself everything else can be taken for granted—conveniently forgetting, of course, that what is taken for granted is nobody's concern, and what is nobody's concern will be dealt with by those who don't care.

We like to think that politics is predictably accessible, available when we want it. The sea of politics is an American mare nostrum, across which we can confidently bob in brightly colored containers: elections, replete with flags, colorful advertising, and little moralistic tableaux of the current virtues, all for public instruction. This insures, so the myth goes, that especially at the national level, we the people are implementing what we believe—free choice, majority rule, a unified nation, progress. Lest we be thought to be manipulable or unsophisticated, we are even adroitly aware that the electioneers are trying to manipulate us. We amuse ourselves with their revelations of what goes on behind their own theatrics—polls, campaign finances, plots, and stratagems. Since these secrets are revealed, we seem to think that we can assume that being in the audience is not much removed from actually directing things. No sweat. Safe politics has always been there and always will be. The guys involved in it are just a bunch of bozos who are managing to pick up a few bucks while they hang out at the political circus. The sovereign voters (if they vote) are in charge, directing things. The mere detail, the humdrum running of things, especially by local government, can be left to a safely subservient "they." "They" take care of the "nuts and bolts." Simple, right?

Local government—the words themselves carry the sense of things anonymous and infinitely replicable, the mere "nuts and bolts" of governance. Nuts and bolts. The repeated phrase does what snap characterizations are supposed to do—stop conversation. And when conversation stops, thinking stops, too. But then thinking's not necessary at this level, right? Thinking's not needed for petty detail, for routine, for limited, parochial things. Local government is like the back corner of the hardware store with its bins and shelves of regularly sized, identical fasteners—always there and always the same. Plenty of people use the phrase. It elicits automatic agreement: Yeah. The nuts and bolts. No need to question or think or learn; it's just the same old stuff. We already know all about it.

What this commonplace prejudice misses is this: it doesn't feel that way when you do it. Actually *do* it. Not just observe or talk or criticize or make another sweeping judgment from in front of the television set. When one sets about doing it, it's not at all like mere detail. But trying to challenge so firmly set a characterization, no matter how wrong it seems, must be foolish. People are interested in "big" things—what color dresses the president's wife prefers, the thickness of a candidate's eyebrows, predictions of the end of the world, ringing pronouncements by celebrities. The "little" stuff—how a governmental budget can be made to work, how a particular person who happens to be a good teacher winds up in a specific classroom, what to actually do about the problem down the street—is mere detail, something for "them" to take care of.

If what we say has no connection with what happens, then silence would be best. Let the show go on, since "they" will be there, taking care of the details, making sure that it all works. But what we say, what we point to and talk about, has a lot to do with what we pay attention to. In turn, what we do pay attention to guides and defines our actions. If governing is to be public and conscious, we have to talk about it in terms that make sense to someone trying to do it, perhaps at the mundane level of "nuts and bolts." Otherwise, carrying on the public's business, even at the level where it is most accessible, becomes the private property of those who do it, while everyone else says irrelevant things about it.

The following account of what governing can mean to those who do it draws on my own experience as a member of the city council of a small, southern manufacturing city. The city and the individuals are described in anonymous terms, but there is little that was secret about the matters described. Initials are used for people's names, but in no pattern. The same person is occasionally labeled with different initials; the same initial can indicate different people. Those involved will recognize some of the events as matters of record, but this is in no sense "the" record. It is an account of things that seemed significant in themselves; how they have been grouped is mostly an afterthought, not the working out of a method.

Such a narrative could not be based on the customary categories and classifications. Instead, I have drawn on my own experience, as directly as possible: what I saw happening, what others said happened, what I thought was really there, all through the distorted lens of my own perceptions. To convey this it is necessary to tell stories, to try to set down accurately what other people said, to describe events and people and places in terms that let them speak for themselves. I must try to find metaphors and illustrations that connect thinking and doing in government and at that place in democracy where people with limited patience for textbook answers can call you at home, stop you on the street, or approach you in a store to ask questions or tell you what they think.

There is another reason not to be very specific about names, dates, and empirically definable particulars. What follows aims at showing the lived world of face-to-face politics and governance, so its distinctive trait must be a consciously personal perspective on public matters. No one can take this as a final, "true" account of things that happened in Hill City. The city will speak for itself, anyway.

But then what value can there be in an account that does not claim to replicate the "truth" of the matter, that does not rely on the customary assurance of having followed a strictly defined method as its claim to authority? Simply this: for governance to be something other than what is mutely, stupidly *there* (like a rock or the tide), both observers and participants must apprehend the inner sense of what doing the activity is like. This inner sense shouldn't be pigeonholed as a matter of irrational "intuition" or, worse, a murky aggregation of impressions casually labeled "wisdom." It has a truth of its own that warrants more examination than it is generally given. Though it seldom happens, the sense can be made available for those willing to join a dialogue about it.

To try to set such a conversation going, I will describe some events and reports of events as I encountered them. Since a full description requires that I also be aware of the limits of my perceptions, which I can never fully be, I have set myself an ultimately impossible task. Oddly enough, to acknowledge at the outset that the journey I am undertaking may not be completed doesn't concern me much. I am comforted by the thought that a pilgrimage need not reach its goal to be worth the effort, that much may be encountered and learned along the way.

What follows necessarily draws on many different kinds of sources. Clear, competent technical reports, prepared according to exacting professional standards, are utter necessities for the governing of even our small city. But there are also necessary places for educated guesses, hunches, community lore, wildly subjective personal preferences, and night thoughts about fate, destiny, and God's purposes. The result is intended to be not an exposition but an invitation. An invitation sets a beginning point. It may even establish an initial direction, but the results depend on who responds and what they do. Perhaps some may come to recognize their own untapped capacities for citizenship.

ONE

•

Praxis

Work the work which the gods ordained for men.

—Hesiod, *Works and Days*

My office's north windows have a magnificent view. Three stories up from the top of a hill, they look out over a quarter of the city to the blue masses of the mountains beyond. In the winter, when the leaves are off the trees, I can see some of the old, red tin roofs looming up along streets laid out two generations ago. The big, rambling houses they belong to are not mansions and were never the homes of the mighty or even the well known; they were just large, frame structures that aimed more at containing space than keeping out the cold or the heat or whatever. Houses built for merchants or clerks or maybe even factory foremen and their large families, they are hard to sell now and don't bring much. The trees that screen them, tall but not really that old, soften the signals of decay: a sagging porch here, peeling paint there, some poorly re-pointed chimneys.

The old photographs of these neighborhoods give a different impression. Even in a blurred print, the landscape still looks sharper and more stark than it does today, almost desert-like in its treelessness, and the houses appear startlingly new and angular. The streets on which the houses were built look as if they were drilled straight as rifle bores across the hillsides and then lined precisely with strips of curb and sidewalk. Our sentimental perception of comforting, ordinary, grandparental abodes slips away, revealing something harsh and assertive. They weren't always there, they were *made,* imposing an urban order on the old farms, the meandering rural roads, and the scattered population.

The old photos don't show the water mains and sewers running under the new streets, but there are photographs taken during the construction of that era's new reservoir up in the mountains, showing the crews at work and the slow growth of the monolithic concrete dam. How much did these laborers know, pausing a moment for the camera before they turned back to work? Thin, hard men with picks and shovels and wooden wagons pulled by mules—men and animals of sweat, dust, and wrinkles, consecrating their labor to a smooth, geometrical, concrete cage for a lake. Built at an altitude of one thousand feet, the dam would make possible the gravity-fed delivery of mountain water to a storage tank on the highest hill in the city—eight hundred feet above sea level. But what did they think of whatever white-shirted dude came up from town in a buggy, bringing a camera all that way only for a few snaps of the shutter? Maybe the men thought they were just doing a job, just one more way to make . . . what? A dollar a day?

Then again, maybe some of them shared, no more than dimly, as their old familiar tools shaped something new and strange, the engineers' bright faith in progress, in man's capacity to transform his life and his world. The reservoir and the twelve-mile-long aqueduct to town replaced the old system that pumped water from the river. Clear, pure, mountain water— for the entire city. Eight million gallons a day! And this was no indulgence; surely there was a well-understood apprehension of what the meticulous, bureaucratic health officials would later report: the number of typhoid fever cases was reduced by nearly two-thirds. No statistic has meaning of its own: which of the men in this photograph had watched someone in his house die of typhoid, vomiting and delirious after a week of high fever?

The old system itself had been the brilliant accomplishment of the city a lifetime earlier. The new system was not just progress but part of a *history* of progress. The city had been aware of it each step of the way, expressing it in lofty terms in the 1827 report of the Common Council Watering Committee: "May not the Corporation [the municipal corporation, the City] . . . by the successful achievement of this important work, so highly conductive to the health, happiness, and safety of her own citizens . . . point the way to her sister towns . . . , to the attainment of similar blessings." They were conscious of what they were doing, and the undertaking turned out to be a success when the system was completed two years later, the third such system completed in the United States, the first in the South, the equal of Philadelphia's. . . .

Something else—a late afternoon phone call after a day busy with other things. The January rain clouds were so low that all I could see outside was the line of trees down the hill; the city and mountains were lost in the dark mist. It was a political call, at least ostensibly, from J., about the problems of the privately endowed library. I had no answer to give, but offered some agreeable murmuring: "Yes, sad situation, not really in the city's hands. . . ." J. was retired, quite old I think, his engineering firm now a very considerable business. He was tall, only a little stooped, and with strong, distinctive features—must have cut a hell of a figure when he was younger. He seemed to want to talk as well as complain about the deterioration and vandalism of the short train in one of the parks—such a shame when it had been so carefully assembled from several railroads. He harked back to more promising times, his voice strengthening as he firmly recounted the names of those who had occupied seats of honor on the little train as it was switched from the Southern's main line to the temporary track to the park. His voice sped up. He went on to recall the exact length of the track, the length of time that the railroad's main line was cut, who donated the protective fence around it once the train was installed, and more. The conversation went on as the gray mist outside turned black. We had met often enough, always cordially, but had never had an extended conversation like this, certainly not an intimate one. I murmured, "Yes, it's a shame people don't appreciate the history behind these things." Suddenly, his real voice, his old one from however many years back, strong and clear, boomed out his instant response, "And if they don't know the *history* of it, they can't know the *meaning* of it!" For one startling moment, the old man's querulous list of complaints, criticisms, and hopes gone awry vanished. The archetypal engineer, the onetime local personification of the profession, rose to philosophy. (That voice—how many green Tech students had been whipped into shape by it?)

"The meaning of it!" Even that first water system of 150 years ago had had something of the adroit and technological about it: a novel pump design, doubled efficiency, the power of the river itself raising water 242 feet up the hill. It was a triumph of hydraulic engineering at the time, unquestionably, and the work on it began with a celebration, a civic festival. The local rifle and artillery companies led a parade to the site of the proposed pumping station for the laying of the cornerstone—a genuine stone, an actual part of the building. According to the local newspaper, the military units were followed by "the Rev. Clergy, the Engineer, the members of the common council preceded by the watering committee," more notables, the Masonic fraternity to lay the cornerstone, and still more. There were speeches, music, and prayers. The hillside around was "thronged with spectators."

The headline for the newspaper account of the affair read simply, "Interesting Event!" Does that sound odd? Was it possibly a tacit admission that the paper sometimes printed accounts of uninteresting events? *Interesting*—strange to find the newspaper inviting attention to a matter and not presuming to offer, godlike, the distilled essence, the "reality" of it. Maybe partisan journalism—if there were enough journals to cover most sides—was better. Odd, too, that the article started with a blast at the state's backwardness (a Whig paper in a Whig town in a Democratic state in 1828) and devoted most of the space to reprinting the speech given by the Watering Committee chairman. It was a good speech, informative and coherent, with just enough boosterism to remind the audience of the reality of civic competition.

I had heard that the water department still had a piece of the first iron pipe—over 150 years old—and I asked to see it. Their conversation is easy to imagine: "A council member wants to see . . . what?" "C'mon, humor 'em a little. It's up there somewhere." What would it look like? Black with age, pitted, something else? I got the predictable treatment, respectful and a little wary. They softened a bit when they understood I wasn't scalp-hunting. One of them actually said, "We want to make a little museum, but right now this stuff is just stored up here."

It was a strange procession—the department director and a displaced council member in suits and ties, flanked by a covey of technicians in work clothes, picking their way through the underused rooms that amounted to the water department's attic, cluttered with old records, lengths of pipe, bags of something or other, meters, measuring devices. The heirloom pipe I sought was in a corner, hidden by other stuff. One of the men wrestled things out of the way and there it was, in a well-kept wood and glass case. The ancient sample of pipe—sent to Philadelphia for the United States Centennial in 1876—clean, gray, and grainy looking, a perfectly ordinary, seemingly new piece of cast-iron pipe. "Seven inch pipe. They don't make that any longer." We all stood silent, a little awkward. What in hell did all this accomplish? The director sensed I wanted an impression of antiquity, something crusted and defective. Despite the light rain we went outside and walked through a dumping yard where some scaled and rusted valves and lengths of worn-out pipe were waiting for final disposal, but the only message conveyed by the junk was that a water system, once constructed, must be continually reconstructed.

On Saturday, June 19, 1829, the new system—dam, canal, pump, supply main, and reservoir—was ready for testing. Both the chairman of the Watering Committee and a clergyman on the city council who had been a strong supporter of the project were warned to leave town when the system failed as the local skeptics had predicted. (Of course, the river couldn't be expected to raise its own water up to that height, and the scoffers, as always, were going to have some fun when this expensive fantasy wrecked on the rocks of reality.) The signal was given, and the pump started. In the spirit of empirical research, a boy was lowered on a rope into the supply main—nothing but a far-off roar, and he was pulled back up. Down a second time—blowing dust and a rumble, and up he came again. The third time down he heard the hiss and burble of the upcoming water and let out a yell of his own. They yanked him out and the water rushed up after him, filling the reservoir.

Over a century later, children reenact the scene in school pageants. Why? What purpose could such an expression of civic remembrance serve? Perhaps a recalling of the town's "height of times," when it led the way, when the chairman of the Water Committee envisioned not just the project, but what the town might become—a center of industry and enterprise, "the place of largest [tobacco] inspection in this country"?

The chairman's speech still reads well, but he was not a charismatic leader. One gossipy observer described him as "a plain, middle-aged man, pale-faced and very distant in his manner." He was a prosperous craftsman and merchant who spent most of his civic energy not on politics but on promoting the growth of the Methodist Church. He was a success by most standards, and a century later a grandson, a bank president bearing his name, served on yet another committee that oversaw a portion of one of the later improvements to the system. But the family name is gone from today's phone book—none left. What can we make of either the chairman or the town, especially that crowd of witnesses that gathered on the hillside at the dedication, watching the militia units and the gathered notables—not just celebrities, but men of actual weight in town matters?

The establishment of a novel and significant public utility, in this case, had little of the utilitarian about it. The shrewd, intense, religious zealot who urged the town to an exultant belief in its own future was moved by convictions deeper than the rational calculation of advantage, even though the improvement *was* a net advantage. Nor did anybody set a goal, then calculate the means necessary to reach it. It was awareness of the *possibility* of doing what had not been done, possibility in the full, practical sense of the word, that set the inspirers of the project apart from the detractors. No idealist chose among fantasies then tried to see if the choice could be made to work in the "real" world, and no one rallied the public by simply pointing out that science and technology proved it could be done. It was "pure water at every door" and "security against the ever threatening calamity of fire, the necessities of the town and a due regard to our own safety and comfort" that gave meaning to the little settlement's efforts to push itself further along what "the discerning Jefferson" himself, the chairman pointed out, had said was the town's "correct course."

"The discerning Jefferson"—who better for Whigs to cite as an *authority*? Let the yokels in the crowd who think the forces of "nature" will do what needs doing fight their way around that name. It was politics, yes, but rhetoric, too, and public ceremony in its service. And tangled up with all of that was an informed, qualitative judgment about the state of the art in hydraulic engineering, the capacity of the town to pay for the project, and the public reaction to the completed project. Could anything have been done—actually brought about—without all of these? Distressing, or maybe not, this shortage of identifiable utilitarians in the neighborhood of the public utilities. It could be an accident or a simple joke, played by Descartes's evil genius, or experimental error, clouding our perceptions. Is it possible that the other communities that followed suit did so without bands and parades, no sense of, "If they can afford it, we'd better get . . . ," no other local merchant in league with another forceful young clergyman, whipping public opinion along? Maybe the rest *were* rational calculators of advantage, quietly totting up the estimated gains and only afterward deciding to move forward. Maybe. But it's hard to visualize, especially at the start of something. The utilitarian approach is suited to the doing of something well-established, the work of minds in the *certeris paribus* habit that don't need (or want) to adapt to a change in context, that can't even conceive of how to answer the challenge of, "Why?" "Why are we doing this?" "What does this mean?"

J.'s voice again, almost seeming to come out of the gloom and the rain instead of out of the telephone receiver: "If they don't know the history of it, they can't know the meaning of it!" Whatever the "it" is, if "they" take it as just a thing that is there, something fixed and permanent, not part of the unfolding record of human effort, then something is lost for all, and something more is lost than whatever is degraded by the affront to those who planned and worked and tried, only to find that what they wrought was no longer seen as a human project at all. The greatest damage is done to the beholders, who forego their own sense of human power, their own sense of what can be done and how.

Let's try something else, some other human action with human consequences, possibly not an everyday necessity. Probably then we can recover our sense of reality. After all, isn't that the purpose of most inquiry, to reconfirm what we already know? Surely what we loosely call "pragmatism" hasn't been reduced to a tattered quilt that we hang on to merely for comfort. Quantity can be a standard for judgment, can't it? If we can produce five million gallons of water a day, ten million is better, not to mention twenty or forty million, right? But no more of water.

It was a slow night at the police station. Not a good choice if a lot of action was to be important—a Monday, the second week of the month, and cool and rainy on top of it. So the watch commander and the ride-along council member (me) hung out at the station for a little while. He showed me the computer terminal and printer, perched on a government-surplus-looking table in the inner alcove of the office. There was not much grant money for computers in those days—this one was a slightly grimy monument to the salad days of the Law Enforcement Assistance Administration and all that. Next to it was a wall with shelves for more traditional equipment—some protective helmets, a wheel for measuring distances (painted bright red, not its first coat of paint) propped up in the corner.

The officers, particularly the older two, seemed an odd contrast to the worn, institutional surroundings: hair carefully cut and brushed, shoes shining, uniforms neat and clean, the badges and patent leather equipment belts gleaming. "This thing saves a lot of work." There was a happy note in his voice as he set to work on the keyboard to demonstrate the record-keeping program. He wanted to show how he could keep track of his men, a little self-consciously following the manual. Officer M.'s record came up on the screen—last month's arrests. A few more than sixty, all told. "Take a look at that." He pointed to thirty or so arrests in the single category of "speeding arrests assisted by radar." "That's okay. Those are easy arrests to make. If he had sixty it wouldn't be good. But he's a good officer. He'll go after the hard ones. Back in the old days, we used to have a CAT can— Catch A Thief. Everybody'd put a quarter in, and the next guy to catch a thief in a building would win the pot. Got as high as fifty dollars—that was money in those days. And catching someone inside a building ain't easy." He turned toward me with a knowing smile.

A few officers went in and out of the adjoining office. C. came in, and they talked some more about the word processor. "Saves time. Used to do all the record-keeping by hand—once a month. Took nine hours, then times three for each shift. . . ." Earlier he had talked about the changes since he started police work—tighter supervision, more stress, fewer opportunities to "goof off and never have anybody know."

I had asked the chief for some time with a watch commander, and he had assigned me to S., a good choice, who just kept talking to give me a feel for his job. He commented about his career ("Twenty years of police work is enough for anyone") and about the officers generally. He seemed to have a special interest in the youngest ones—his own children were starting careers, so maybe he could be expected to be especially sensitive to the officers in their early twenties who were making far greater commitments than they realized. There was a pool table in the room the officers passed through at shift-change times. "I like to see the young ones play pool—they'll joke around and laugh a lot. But after two years or so that stops. They get quieter. I guess by then they've seen so much it affects 'em. Or maybe they're just older." Earlier he had discreetly lobbied me for higher starting salaries. Fair enough—the budget was coming up, and I'd opened myself to the opportunity. . . .

We passed some more time at the word processor, calling up records of this and that. Intersections with the most accidents, intersections with the worst accidents; I pocketed the printout for later use in a zoning dispute. We called up the record of calls to the police for the street I lived on. Not many. "Boy, you live on a *quiet* street!" To prove it wasn't totally quiet, I recalled the time A. and I inadvertently rescued a riding lawn mower from a joy-riding rustler. Hearing the clatter and roar in the street late one summer night, we had both switched on our outside lights within seconds of each other, startling the felon into fleeing, leaving his loot, engine still running, in the middle of the street. A. got a couple of beers and we sat on the evidence, providing testimony to the investigating officers when they finally got there, until they eventually determined that the paddy wagon was the most convenient vehicle to haul the evidence downtown. They lifted it in with the back of the mower toward the front of the truck. Our last sight of it was the reflection of its headlights, visible through the little window in the door, looking for all the world like the sorrowful eyes of some figure in a children's book being unjustly taken to jail.

Story time over. We went to check on the new dispatching operation: police combined with fire and emergency (under some duress from the council). The new E911 system would give everyone more to do. S. chuckled about the fire dispatchers having to become accustomed to the continued intensity of police dispatching. Back to the squad car and more driving.

We went out to check the airport. There were no planes in. It was quiet, actually in the county's jurisdiction. Earlier he had said, "Something happening to kids—I've never gotten used to that. Something happens, and it'll be a while before I go to sleep that night." But this remained a quiet night, not even a backup on a "domestic." Not like the last time. That one had been with a younger officer on the downtown beat, a Friday night in late summer that reached its finale with the prevention of a suicide, and that after a greasy, indigestible meal at a hamburger place, then theft calls, traffic violations, and a neighborhood fight. The officer had been tense—my being along couldn't have helped any, but I was so nervous myself I barely realized it. He had managed to have the investigation of a rock-throwing incident turn into a midstreet wrangle with the drunken husband of the putative victim, attended by a large portion of this still-white inner-city street, two police backups, and an ambulance. The neighbors had been summoned by the daughter of the family, a beautiful young woman with blue eyes and black hair, who stood in the street screaming repeatedly, "He's drunk as shit, and they're putting *handcuffs* on him!" The rock throwers, unidentifiable "niggers on bicycles," were never caught. The only one arrested was the husband, who seemed to be no stranger to the police station.

No such drama this night. Having contented ourselves that the airport offered little prospect of excitement, we drove over a new section of road— a feeder for the section of the new bypass that was scheduled next for construction. "See? Look at that. You can't see who's coming this way!" The intersection of an old road and the new one was badly crowned. "Someone needs to take care of that before the construction is finished. That can really be dangerous." "Hmm. Yeah. Have to check it out." We were out on the portion of the bypass that had been completed; there was little traffic. A couple of radio transmissions broke the silence—a routine automobile license check, an officer looking for papers for a report that he had to finish. The bypass's pavement was wet, and the tires hissed as we sped along. Then we were off the bypass and driving through a blue-collar neighborhood, talking about the state legislature's decision to raise the drinking age and how that would create new law-enforcement problems. Neither of us had much taste for more hassles with young people—there were enough as it was. And as it turned out, each of us had a weak stomach that foiled our otherwise enthusiastic taste for hard liquor—both of us saved from alcoholism by our infirmities?

We traveled down the midtown expressway and out Main to the Boulevard. The rain had stopped, and the streets were dry. The tires just hummed. Little else, just the black ribbon of road repeatedly punctuated by the blue glares of the streetlights. We went around the back of the last shopping center. No problem with the lights still being on there; so-and-so often stayed late at his business. Then the dramatic action of the night: a dead cat on Catawba Road. "Don't look at the light." He switched on the spotlight to get a house number, then called in a low voice, almost mumbling into the microphone, "Center? Dead animal in the street at 4130 Catawba Road." And that was all. No backup calls, no other officers needing assistance, no felonies, no automobile accidents, no "domestics." I hadn't wanted the Friday night, payday, end-of-month, full-moon, hot-weather civil nightmare, but, as they all said, it was *very* quiet. Typically quiet, a night of catching up on small leftover pieces of work, of waiting, of boredom and worry over what would break the boredom. S. made one last observation before we turned down my street. "Sometimes I think I'd like to be a psychologist and get into the minds of cops, find out why they do it." A pause. "Sure must be strange."

What then of police work? We expect officers to take community college courses in "police science"; we expect them to be trained and know the techniques of their vocation. They work by rigid rules and to be effective must be continually mindful of the law, the restrictions both on people generally and on themselves. Does this make the work a technology, the application to practice of the "principles" discovered by "police science," computer-assisted, college-taught, credentialed?

Maybe. But other, stranger things present themselves. They care for a community they come to understand by worrying about the sight distances at a new intersection and by absorbing a myriad of details about its life, down to who works late at his business and where what kind of automobile accident occurs. If the discipline of the officers is maintained in part by meticulous records and modern data-processing, the judgments they point to still boil down to knowing who's a good enough cop to catch someone inside a building and wondering why the younger officers stop horsing around at the pool table after two or three years. And it's capped off by reflecting, late at night at the end of an inconsequential shift driving a politico around, why someone would do it.

What we are pleased to call our "system of law enforcement" turns out to be the work that cops do. Despite the efforts to render all these things in impersonal, technical, mechanical terms that convey some illusion that these things happen in conformance with the grand laws of the universe, it is still a matter of who does it and what they think of themselves while they're doing it.

But how about arrest rates, complaints, clearances, public opinion polls?

Surely we can make judgments—final, authoritative judgments—in their terms, can't we? And can't we prove that qualitative judgments can be securely based on quantitative reports? The alternative is certainly unpleasant enough: being absolutely required to assess relationships and characters, immersing ourselves in the complex exchanges of meaning that surround concrete activities, accepting coresponsibility for such nebulous things as "setting the tone" of public life.

Here is another alternative, then. Politics itself will afford us (won't it?) the chance to be comfortably technical. After all, politics is will, power, and the transmission of that power, isn't it? A matter of mechanics through and through, safely reducible to calculation, the count at the ballot box, a public opinion poll—right? Said to myself: "Well, crap. That's no help."

I know better than to open the mail before supper, especially the predictable political stuff. This time, it was a form letter, sent to everyone on the council, beginning with the salutation, "Dear Sir." It deserved to be answered with a form letter beginning with "Dear Jerk," for trying to influence a decision by insulting everyone—typical of the self-righteous nerds who unleash themselves when they wake up long enough to find out something may affect them. The killer line in this one read, "What will you be thinking of? Money or the concerns and wishes of the people who you serve?" I wouldn't let it affect me; after all, I'd been working for six weeks to try to accomplish what this character wanted to happen—the rejection of a rezoning that had been approved by the Planning Commission. Now he made the job harder; at least two of those who may have been on the fence could well vote in favor of the damned thing just to show what they think of this kind of style—or, rather, lack of it.

The rezoning was predictable enough—from residential to heavy commercial, on the most heavily traveled piece of road in town and at the second worst intersection for traffic accidents. The Planning Commission approval surprised me; it was my ward, so as soon as the paper published their decision I was in the saddle. The first step had been to call the neighborhood organizer who had not prevailed at the Planning Commission; pleasantly, he had been getting ready to call me and was happy at being contacted. He didn't say so, but I'd be willing to bet he was relieved at not having to make the call, trying to figure out how he would be received. Callers, at least the ones I've had any contact with, tend to fall into one of two categories: the supplicants, full of elaborate courtesy, dropping names, flattering as they go; and the avenging angels, full of righteous wrath and carrying such an emotional head of steam that it must take them a couple of hours to work themselves up to actually dialing the number.

Happily for me, this one was well organized and practical; he understood that he was trying to achieve a result, not undertake a Manichean mission to identify the pure good and the pure evil in the universe. He liked the approach I suggested, and we agreed that a preliminary meeting would be the way to start.

A couple of days later, a couple of calls made. A dozen or so people from the neighborhood came to the meeting, held at a church that was itself outside the city limits, set well back from the road in a grove of oak trees, almost invisible in the darkness. For me, it was another night out. I went down the long drive, around back onto the fresh gravel of the parking lot. There were ten or so cars already there, parked under the dusk-to-dawn light.

The little group was assembled in one of the clean, neat, Sunday-school rooms—folding chairs and tables, light gray asphalt tile floor, still lighter walls and ceiling. I recognized a couple of them—W. retired now, and another older man I hadn't seen in a while. I was introduced to the others, carefully, pleasantly, one at a time. It was a good mix—men and women, older and younger. The two older women carefully identified themselves as widows.

Finally, the meeting began: first, a review of the problem was presented. The Planning Commission—why did they do it? The developer had been smooth and skillful; the hearing room small. The traffic, the intersection . . . one of the men at our meeting was the husband of a woman who had been in an accident at the intersection a couple of years before. I felt good that I remembered the name and the event; that established, he seemed less on guard. It was a good meeting—maybe even better than good. The young man who organized it had organized his materials, too—a map, a report from consulting engineers, and more. He understood and had helped the others grasp that they had to make a case, that demands and denunciation were not the way to work it. That done, I did my part.

My role, at this meeting, was practiced; not like the first time I led a meeting, with the fractious group from the pretty blue-collar neighborhood. Most people fear government and fear officials; they react to official settings the way I react to hospitals, I guess. So I went through a typical council meeting's procedure, explained the council chamber's physical arrangement, did a little role-playing walk-through: "Be yourself, say something straightforward; don't be afraid to say how it will affect you personally. . . ."

As usual, they seemed more encouraged and more at ease. Then the political self-assessment came: I listed the council members and asked, "OK, who do you know?" Sure enough, among the group of twelve, individual members had contacts of some kind with almost every one of the seven council members. They became a little more confident; they took some time sorting out who would contact whom. "Don't bombard them, but be firm and clear." "Let's get 'em out here to look at this mess during rush hour." "Yeah, and . . ." It went on. Nearly all the council members were to be called by someone who knew them.

It ran for over an hour and a half, counting travel time, taking more than two hours of my evening. We agreed to break up, and we put the chairs back in the Sunday-school arrangement. If I left first, it would give them a chance to talk among themselves and decide if they really liked the whole approach or not. One of the older women made sure she spoke to me on my way out: "It was certainly a pleasure to meet with our representative." That was an odd way for her to put it—or was it? I'd never heard it put that way before. Well, it was nice enough . . . no, really nice. They filed out right behind me; there was no need to consult without me in the room. Not a bad night at all. . . .

There was a good sign at the next council meeting: the organizer was there, watching and taking notes. He was smart enough to have done his homework. S. would never have handled them this way; he would have made a little speech, told them how he would pull strings and do them a bunch of favors—with the implicit message that a favor performed is a debt, subject to later redemption. That's not my style, anyway. It's better to try to give them some sense of how to make things work on their own and hope they remember who encouraged them. Another night of . . . what? Doing well politically by doing political good? Making democracy work?

Postscript: The zoning proposal was turned down by the council in a rare reversal of the Planning Commission. From the composition of the crowd at the meeting, a bunch of the real-estate people had evidently decided to view this particular request as a test case. And after the battle (middling-sized, out-of-town commercial investment in choice land versus neighborhood opposition, traffic problems, government control) resulted in a loss for what they regarded as "their" side, the grumbling from their forces was audible. T. surfaced again with his predictable line about council being antibusiness, still bristling over having lost two tries at a rezoning effort of eight and nine years earlier. He had wanted residential land across from a school rezoned for heavy commercial use. After he spoke, there was murmuring from some others.

They must have really gotten excited when several months later we appointed the young man who had led the neighborhood protest to a seat on the Planning Commission. The member from that part of town had to retire at the end of his term, and there were no obvious candidates for the seat—the noticeable old-timers were probably not interested in educating themselves about land-use planning, and the younger ones were too busy with family and business. So we appointed him, to look out for the neighborhood as much as anything else, and maybe spare us a few head-aches. Hollywood ending: A couple of years later, another request to re-zone the same piece of land passed, this time to a more moderate commer-cial use—a furniture showroom for a local concern, with an attractively landscaped site plan, and minimum interference with the neighborhood. The neighborhood man on the Planning Commission voted for it (he turned out to be a moderate, conscientious as well as intelligent), and the council agreed, to the accompaniment of expressions of praise for the firm's com-mercial acumen and local statesmanship.

Where does this leave us in understanding the work of governing? The public utilities turn out to be founded on the commitments of visionaries, and the drama and violence of police work seem to be based on a regard for peace and reasonable order by officers who are almost hypersensitive to the seemingly countless pieces of the community's human mosaic. Even pol-itics and (flourish of trumpets, a lowering of voices a couple of octaves to impress everyone with the *seriousness* of it all) government decision-making are not the neatly separable "decisions" of legend. Instead, one concern blends into another—a denial can become palatable and explicable if it is eventually followed by an affirmation, and the affirmation is not a reversal of the earlier denial if it contains within itself an illumination of the earlier decision: yes, believe us, more cars on a large number of "in-and-out" trips are a burden on an overcrowded street; believe us, private investment can be made in ways that make public sense. And if one decision blends into another, mingling and intertwining until decisions about land use become decisions about appointments and highway construction and neighbor-hood organization, what about the "information" on which "decisions" are "based"? Technical information—strict, mathematical, objective infor-mation about traffic counts, rush-hour flow, the distance available for exit lanes, the probable effect of a new traffic light on an intersection where the older light has failed to regulate the traffic—is necessary. But that's not enough. There are more questions: Do the big semi-trailers really speed through there, running red lights? Have the police patrolled the area and made an appropriate number of arrests? If they have, why are people afraid? ("Remember that accident Mrs. B. was in? . . .")

These questions are not separable from a quiet, businesslike, neighborhood meeting, where two of the older women introduce themselves as widows to say . . . what? Possibly: "My husband, who would have been the one to do this sort of public thing, is dead and cannot speak for me or make sure that the car runs smoothly anymore, so I have to come here myself, though what I've done for years is keep a clean, pleasant home, raised my children and not been a pushy, loud-mouthed woman. I'm here because I have to be. The house is most of what I've got, and I'm afraid of more changes, more traffic, more . . ."

Those who imagine government and politics—public life—to be something different, something remote from personal life, are wrong. In their imaginations they turn the difference between public and personal into the difference between ordinary and extraordinary. What a comforting idea—an extraordinary life existing right alongside the humdrum, run-of-the-mill, daily routine! Like an Australian aborigine's spirit world, it supposedly exists alongside us, but unseen, and filled with strange, unknowable powers that must either be appeased so they don't bring disaster upon us or else be coaxed into intervening on our behalf, bringing us power over rain or victory or whatever from the unseen other world.

That's an odd way to see things when we live in what likes to style itself a democracy, where we go so far as to inform ourselves of even the intimate details of the president's personal health. Unless in all the trivia, in all the mass-media presentations about and public reactions to personalities in high office, there are no properly political lessons at all. Maybe in our surfeit of information about what we cannot affect, we have neglected to remind ourselves about how to deal with what we can affect and so have lost sight of politics as the work of having a community. Politics, by being made to be something "other," something extraordinary, seems no longer to be something we do, but simply something that happens.

The onerous part of having a democracy is that so much depends on someone paying attention to details, on those involved having some skill at negotiation among equals, on there being a willingness to accept coresponsibility for matters that cannot be fully controlled. It is easy to understand the relief of believing that there is a place where decisions can be made in a complete and self-contained way, like Jehovah ordering, "Let there be light." But human command is never complete and self-executing; believing otherwise is simply a way to avoid confronting the inevitable.

Governing is an activity, not a belief. If it is not done one way, it will be done another. Like all activity it involves work, and the physicists teach us that work is the product of effort and time. Its essence is commitment and persistence, not dazzling revelations or the intrusion of other worlds into this one or even "neat ideas." The perceptions of those efforts, their objects and consequences, how their long seasonal rhythms are punctuated by bursts of intensity, are further matters.

TWO

•

Symbol

Burial of the dead is perhaps the fundamental phenomenon
of becoming human.

—Hans-George Gadamer, *Reason in the Age of Science*

After the funeral I talked to several people who had been moved to tears
when they saw the firemen at Firehouse Number Three standing at attention in the rain. The police, of course, had played the major parts in the
procession—pallbearers, honor escorts, and traffic guards who blocked the
streets so that the hearse and the cars of the mourners could roll from
church to cemetery in a long, unbroken file. (If you don't want your
funeral procession sprinkled with teenagers in hot rods and lost tourists,
die a retired police commander and member of the city council.) But the
firemen were unexpected. Like the late spring thunderstorm that had
swept wind, rain, and the low, ragged clouds over us, they startled and
moved those who were there.

Before the service began, we six surviving members of the council had
gathered in the foyer of the church, but it was hard for me to think of this
as a civic occasion. H. and I had been close, so it was much more personal
for me, and I was preoccupied with my own thoughts. The others gathered and waited to see what duties we might have. K., the newest council
member and a highly placed corporate executive, had misjudged the occasion and worn a light-colored suit. The rest of us had put on our darkest,
most severe clothes, as had most of the crowd in the big church in this
aging but still middle-income neighborhood. The sanctuary itself was
open and airy, built in a Georgian institutional style, and the front was
filled with flowers.

The church was overflowing with mourners, more than a few of them
visibly grief-stricken, making it even harder for me to keep my composure.
H. and his wife had not had children of their own and, as near as I know,
had made up for that by aiding and encouraging a number of relatives from

each of their families—large, old-fashioned rural families with plenty of in-laws and cousins, each with their own share of hopes and problems. I myself had benefited from that quiet willingness to help; maybe that's why I was preoccupied with self-control during the service.

It was certainly a political funeral, but there was nothing cynical about it. H. had meant something not reducible to words, maybe not even expressible except through a large, very formal, public funeral. He had only a high school education, and his career as a police officer had had its setbacks as well as its successes. His strongest supporters tended to be those of his own generation, especially those who had to go to work at an early age, foregoing much schooling as an unaffordable luxury. They seemed to carry a slight contempt for the ease and cosmopolitanism brought by the last thirty years of prosperity, as if convinced deep down that it wouldn't last. H. himself had occupied his spare time in the ancient tasks of gardening and keeping bees. Two or three years earlier the television news people had filmed a remarkably sensitive interview with him, not the usual day-in-the-life-of, know-your-councilman item. They caught him tending his beehives on a late, sunny afternoon, and the television picture was suffused with bright, golden light. When they asked him one of those predictable questions about what he wanted for the city, he gave an answer that was predictable only if you knew him, far from our conventional rhetoric about civics. In the glow of late afternoon, almost in a reverie, and entranced by the timeless productivity of the bees, he said that he wished the people of the city could cooperate the way bees did in the hive, for harmony and productivity. The television camera lingered on him, the sunlight, and the thought. Expressed quietly and optimistically, it was still a deeper and sterner assessment than we generally make, a Spartan view of the city that revealed something lost on most of us: that there can be great honor and achievement in willingly subordinating oneself to the community, which itself would be less if we chose otherwise. Perhaps that too was a part of what was mourned at the funeral—the passing of a capacity for self-discipline that will never be replaced, even if sometime we come to recognize it as something we need.

It was a relief to get back to the car just before the rain started. First, large, deliberate splatters, then the downpour. It was a good thing M. was driving. We squeezed out of the parking lot, and I managed to stay collected until we passed Firehouse Number Three, and then there they were, the uniformed firemen, standing at attention in the rain. The rivalry between the two uniformed services is an old one here, as it is in most places. Police officers will, if prompted, express their clear disdain for the firemen's leisurely life of staying at the firehouse waiting to be called. But the actual loss of life in the line of duty is far greater among the firemen, and it is a fireman's memorial fountain that graces one corner of the old park. Paying homage to a fallen colleague and rival, the firemen stood at attention in the rain.

I found out later that the gesture had affected others the same way it had affected me, and even years later witnesses remembered it. Shortly after the funeral, F. and I had taken a moment to talk about H.'s death and the funeral and the firemen, too: "Did you see the firemen?" "Yeah, I really choked up. It was nice of them to do that." "Yeah, me too." And neither of us spoke for a bit.

That salute displayed a tie between death and civic life, absorbed, if not grasped, by those who sat through the service, jockeyed for places in the line of cars as the rain started, and watched at the graveside as the casket flag (a city casket flag—we had never even had one with the municipal flag design until a few months before, and then we had to use two in one month) was given to the widow and the casket consigned to the red clay. For several days afterward the funeral was a topic of conversation among those who had been a part of the considerable crowd.

His death had been such a shock because he seemed so enduring. When R. died, only four weeks before, we had known it was coming. First, fainting spells, then the diagnosis of brain cancer and the ordeal of radiation treatment and chemotherapy. He had been elected to the council only the year before. But H. had been on the council as long as any of us. He was over six feet tall, with a firm, square frame and large hands and feet. It was hard to imagine anyone he arrested giving him a hard time. He had supported me from the first time I ran for office, sometimes having more confidence in me than I had in myself. He would give me rides to the evening council meetings. When he got to my house he wouldn't honk the horn or come up to the door, but would park at the curb, almost always a minute or two early, and just wait for me to come out. H. was patient and persistent, more than the rest of us, and it unsettled me most to realize that H., in his big blue Mercury, would never pull up in front of the house again. We couldn't help talking among ourselves about how rapidly his death followed R.'s. And for a couple of weeks, street talk was especially solicitous of the rest of us: "Take care of yourself now, we don't need any more council funerals."

No one from the newspaper came to H.'s funeral, at least not that I could see. His death had been covered with the usual story, a nice one, and an editorial tribute was published after a couple of days. But the civic event of the funeral that so struck those who had been there went unremarked in the news. It's strange that death, allegedly bound to come to each of us, is reported as news when it happens, as if it were a surprise. And it's stranger still that funerals—the shared public commemorations of death that politicians, for one group, feel they must attend—are not regarded as news at all. The private portion is grist for publicity; the public portion is treated as if it were private. But of course they wouldn't come. Even here journalism is built on a myth of rationalism, and the awesome facticity of death is a little unsettling to any committed rationalist, including our local ones. Biological death, yes. That's a scientific fact, or a fact that can be described scientifically, or a series of sense data that can be reduced to an idea everyone agrees to call a fact, or something. You can report it without fear of contradiction: message conveyed to receiver, unambiguously, intersubjectively transmissible, sign-stands-for-object. And stop there. Beyond that bare biological observation the signals start to get a little mixed. That's why politicians, those perennial surfers on life's waves of ambiguity, show up at funerals. None of the Republican politicos dared miss it. That's how we knew P. was thinking about running for the congressional nomination—he showed up. But his hypocrisy is irrelevant. He knew, along with the rest of us, something about funerals.

Another anecdote about civic funerals: two black city workers were killed in a freak accident—a flash fire in an enclosed room where they had been working with highly volatile solvent. As mayor, only two months in office, I called on the families, went to the funeral homes, and attended the funerals held in different churches on the same hot August afternoon, humidity so high that by midafternoon thunderheads were building up on this side of the mountains. At each sweltering service—no air-conditioning in either church—each preacher asked me, with no advance notice, to "bring a message on behalf of the city." (Exactly the same words were used in each request.) How could the city government, if only in its role as an employer, justify itself on such an occasion? The answer from John Locke wouldn't do: "They took the job, and I'm sad to report that this is part of what they implicitly agreed to." No, not suitable to use the philosophic ideal of Mr. Jefferson. Nor was it a matter of most anything being said as long as the titular head of the city said it; what was said was important too. Should I say something about the tragedy of life cut short in youth? Both had been young workers. Should I say that the men should serve as reminders to us all? One of the victims in particular had been an example of how advancement toward management was possible for reliable black, blue-collar workers. It was hard to figure out.

I decided to just be content not to lie and maybe try to sound halfway decent, no bombast or efforts to score political points. "Shock . . . tragedy . . . loss to friends and co-workers . . . tried to provide well for those dependent on them. . . ." And without saying anything public about it, I wanted to make sure that the arrangements for insurance payments and workmen's compensation benefits were in order. They were.

Later, a well-known black preacher complimented me for my efforts. At first, I didn't know quite what he was getting at; I realized only later that he hadn't necessarily expected a white mayor to show up at the funerals of two black, blue-collar city workers. I got credit for a decision, but I had never considered not going. At each service, a handful of us city officials were the only whites present. At each we were welcomed warmly and courteously and escorted to places of honor in the front of the church. The ceremonies were elaborate, vigorous, and emotional. In each, the principal bereaved female—widow in one case, pregnant girlfriend in the other—became hysterical about two-thirds of the way through and had to be carried from the church. The remains of the widow's husband were taken to the cemetery of a country church a few miles outside town. We went there, too, as part of the procession. While her small children watched with no understanding at all, the young, slender woman made a frantic, final effort to climb into the grave as two men struggled to restrain her; all this as the sky got hotter and grayer and the first warning gusts of the storm whipped green leaves out of the trees and blew clouds of dust and sand into the departing crowd.

The burnings and deaths of the two workers had been reported in some detail, but the funerals had gotten only the customary notices in the obituaries. Death as a private, concrete fact can be reported publicly, but evidently the news media find it much harder to cover the public experience of something like a funeral. For one thing, it's not a matter merely of observing the externals; the unassisted power of sight fails. Nor is it a subjective matter—X. was solemn, Y. was grief-stricken, Z. was bored. It is both the externals and how we respond to them. The essence of a ceremony is sharing the meaning of what we jointly experience: "Did you see the firemen?" "Yeah. I really choked up. It was nice of them to do that." "Yeah. Me too."

The event becomes more real to those of us who confirm it by sharing it in conversation as well as physical presence; that's precisely what the news people ignore even as they go about making a living trying to change something that is above all a matter of firsthand sharing into something quite different, into one-way "communication." The reality of a true ceremony, the common experience of meaning, cannot be understood merely by looking at it; somehow, one has to be a part of it. Since it's hard to be rational and objective about death, maybe that's why journalists stick to what can be looked at—death-as-biographical-event, the final entry on the résumé. (La Rochefoucauld: "No man can look steadily at death or the sun." In French, the verb *regarder,* to look, with its curious overtone of detachment; *look,* the sense of the observer, not touch, taste, or hearing.)

It may be another of the little deceptions we practice on ourselves to assume that "news" is made up of "observable facts." Real news, tidings, from a person, directly, about something, is composed of more than facts: "This is C. I'm calling from the hospital. H. died just a few minutes ago. We thought he was doing all right, but he must have had a massive heart attack. There were three doctors right there, but they couldn't do anything." I took the call at the kitchen phone in the middle of some other business. We had worried when he had his second heart attack, but the reports had initially been good. Now I could feel the sinking sensation in the pit of my stomach even while I began trying to think of who should be called and in what order.

Or another example: "Ah heered the explosion and saw the fire comin' out the window, an' by then this fella was jes' lying there, cryin'. Doan know how he got that far. We put out the fire on 'em. Poor thing. Looked like a skinned rabbit." We had gone down to see where the explosion and flash fire had happened, a rest room in the old armory—the window out of the room was fifteen feet above the pavement of a former gas station that was being rented for use as a taxi stand by this black man with his thick accent and his wife. Somehow, one of the victims had gotten out of the window and had managed to get thirty-five or forty feet from the building before he collapsed on the concrete.

Meaning is a part of real news. Not in a separate package, but intertwining and permeating those parts of the message that some otherworldly analysts would describe as "data." When the old man who had been helping his wife dispatch taxis talked about the victim looking like a skinned rabbit, he wasn't trying to impress us with a vivid metaphor. The quaver in his voice, the tone of sad resignation, conveyed the genuine terror of the explosion and his sorrow at the reduction of a fellow man to a dying carcass. He drew no attention to having burnt his own hand putting out the fire on the victim. In his phone call, C.'s statement "a few minutes ago" may have been factual, but it was more than a fact. It was a gesture of confidence and respect, the equivalent of, "You're among the first to know," and also a request: "Will you help call those who ought to be notified?"

A question for all of us: If death were just the loss of biological vitality in a single organism, why should anyone count the number of cars in the funeral procession, be comforted that the mayor came and said that the departed had tried hard to provide for those around him, or be shaken by the sight of firemen standing in the rain? And why should anyone talk about it?

Perhaps we should thank death for short-circuiting a lot of the intellectual wiring we tinker with. The vocabulary and norms of contracts, so handy when we chatter about governmental matters, don't apply. We can't try something like, "Well, Death, I don't really see myself going along with this." No, there's not much point in "trying to understand where death's coming from." It comes; it is final. It violates rights and is regularly unfair. It is universal, absolute, and unavoidable. And we don't talk about it much, even though we will all come to it.

Our customary language of politics and government doesn't lend itself to confronting death. Indeed, when we talk about it, we seem to expect that government will forestall or hide it. But while our talk (and writing) about government contents itself with going on about rights to life and the pursuit of happiness, in our actual daily routine we always check the obituaries in the morning paper to see what changes death has made. In response, the city quietly manifests itself in very solid things: the government buildings themselves, the aging monuments, the lesser memorials scattered here and there, the old city cemetery that is occasionally neglected but cared for lovingly when it is tended. It doesn't matter that these reminders of the shortness of our individual lives do not fit with our uncritically held, customary verbal formulations about government and politics. In the solid and the tangible, in what people visit and notice and use, we constantly and easily refer to the tragic part of our civic life. Without apology or explanation, our government surrounds itself with memento mori.

When the city builds a new building, one of the extras that is always added is a bronze plaque. The plaques customarily name in permanent, raised letters the building itself and lists the incumbent members of the city council, headed by the mayor and vice-mayor, as well as the city manager. Some of the older plaques also include the architect and the general contractor and the officials who planned and authorized the project.

It's curious that no one ever complains about the plaques. They cost several hundred dollars apiece, and they certainly aren't required for the public use or the structural integrity of the building. But the company in the next state from which we order the plaques seems to do a good business in them. Their sales brochure doesn't even bother to urge or excite; it consists simply of some photos of work done, descriptions of the twenty-eight plaque sizes, nine letter styles, five border styles, two texture styles, and assurances that full directions will be furnished for mounting. The larger plaques require visible fastenings, rosettes that tastefully disguise the exposed hardware, but the company recommends concealed fastenings to discourage vandalism.

There is an unspoken etiquette that goes with having one's name on a new plaque; it's not good manners to display too much interest in it. At a building dedication, when a plaque is unveiled, a council member doesn't just walk up and stare at his name. The accepted practice is to be more casual about it, to sidle up and look at it obliquely, making sure that the spelling is right and seeing if there are any tacit political messages in the arrangement of the names or the size of the letters, but not so anyone would recognize that that's what you are doing. That we elected officials titillate ourselves with drams of grandeur when we see our names cast in enduring bronze, forever to be read by bored or distracted citizens who happen to be hanging around the entrances of public buildings, is evidently no sin at all in the public eye. Curious, since the same public is pretty quick to spot pretentiousness and exults in deflating it, or maybe not so curious if something is at work besides tinhorn notables inflating themselves at public expense and a bored public refusing to waste its time by putting those officials in their places. The public has its own taste for monuments, and surely it is possible that the habit of public memorials satisfies that taste by touching something far deeper, some almost mysterious resonance between citizen and city. More is at work than deluded vanity; the symbols fascinate us all.

Indeed, a monument is our city's most depicted landmark: a terrace composed of a dramatic set of Italianate steps that plunge down the side of the virtual cliff against which the city was first laid out. The old courthouse, now a museum, is across the street from the top of the steps and draws one's eyes up the steps and to itself. A World War I memorial, dominated by a large "doughboy" statue, is at the bottom, directly on the sidewalk of a busy commercial street. From a distance it's hard to see the relatively simple Confederate statue and memorial at the top of the steps themselves; the statue at the bottom is larger and more dramatic, framed against a large wall that lists the names of all the local dead of the War to End All Wars.

But up close, the Confederate monument is more evocative. In Maine, a number of the villages between Portland and Bar Harbor have identical granite Civil War monuments: statues of soldiers standing stiffly at attention, fully equipped with rifle, kepi, overcoat, and rain cape. They seem to have all come from the same Vermont(?) sculptor, who gave them a curiously vacant look. Our Rebel at the top of the terrace is bronze and weathered. In a slouch hat, with his bedroll over his shoulder, he stands with his feet apart, rifle held lightly in his hands. His face is young and hopeful, and he looks south, his back to the hilltops across the river, now occupied by a gravel pit and a very large mental institution. Taken as a whole, the steps and the statuary are visually dramatic, and representations of them are frequently used in local publications.

But how do these things get here? Did whoever organized all of this have some motive that could be described as something other than selfish? In the case of the names that get listed, is this any more than the authorities giving the survivors of the war-dead a taste of the picayune immortality of the public plaques?

Whatever the motives, the practice is far older than our city, and the vocabulary used to describe the war-dead hasn't changed in two thousand years. The funeral speech that Thucydides put in the mouth of Pericles sounds familiar at the foot of the terrace, in front of the World War I monument: ". . . collectively gave their lives . . . individually received that renown which never grows old . . . their glory is left behind them to be everlastingly recorded. . . ." And there on the wall, facing the busy sidewalk, the names of the dead are listed for any passerby to read. Forty-two in that particular war, including George T. Printup, Jr., Clarence Widdifield, Fred George Geophart, and Pannell Rucker Jones (colored). During the city's big anniversary celebration, the terrace was repaired and monuments listing the dead from World War II, the Korean War, and Vietnam were erected at appropriate places on the landings of the stairway—rather late in catching up, over forty years late in some cases. But the ceremony was elaborate and well attended; middle-aged men who were there wept openly in public.

We even build monuments to do things in. Our new city council chamber has a plain, mostly unornamental decor, but the austerity only serves to heighten the effect of the major ornament in the room—a large, handsome, cast-aluminum city seal, the city government's commemoration of the city itself. It's the old seal, the one with the goddess Ceres on it (or if not that deity of the recognized pantheon, a buxom Victorian lady in a diaphanous gown), and an overflowing cornucopia of the evidences of nineteenth-century local prosperity—a railroad locomotive, tobacco leaves, and the like. Suspended in front of muted blue-gray background drapes in a windowless room, it looms in the gloaming like the head of the Great Oz. When the room was being designed there was some interest in using the newer, abstract "logo" instead of the old seal, but that preference was rejected. Evidently, civic taste is reverting back to recognizable, if fantastic, representations of the city itself, in this case our spirit of capitalism incarnate as sedate earth-mother or whatever.

At the time, the city government was using a different symbol of itself, a stylized logo rather than the official seal, on city vehicles, workers' hard hats, stationery, water bills, and the like. Nor was this a fever of advertising that fell on us alone. Other cities put similar emblems on the same kinds of things. In some places the members of the city council get matching blazers and have patches made in the form of their city emblem sewn on the breast pockets. I have seen these at conventions of city officials; I hope they don't wear them to council meetings at home.

This symbolizing is not merely a matter of display or self-expression; it is also a practical part of having a city government. Having an official seal is one of the legal tests for being a municipality. In the charter of a neighboring city, the General Assembly of the Commonwealth, using a typical phrase, bestowed on that community a "corporate seal and perpetual succession." The fundamental act that created the municipal corporation thus also gave it a collective signature and the power to live beyond the death of any individual citizen. This shouldn't seem unusual. After all, in the British House of Lords, when a new peerage is created and the first occupant comes to the House, he or she is greeted with elaborate ceremony. But when an heir has succeeded to a peerage on the death of an incumbent, there is no ceremony; the new peer merely walks in and takes the seat. The seat is for the peerage, not the individual. When a king of France died, the formula *le roi c'est mort, vive le roi* epitomized the perpetuity of the realm in the face of the mortality of any individual head of it. And in this, our own age of science and materialism, the Russians at one time pickled Lenin himself, making him look as if he had just died, and put him on public display to assure the faithful that the revolutionary moment was with them yet.

A more prosaic instance, not complicated by historical references: in the Tennessee state capitol is a large, old, lever-action stamping machine that can emboss the official state seal. It used to be that if the circumstances were right, a visitor could receive a flat, gold, foil sticker into which he could impress the official state seal by working the machine himself. It was an irresistible attraction, but I don't know if it's still there.

The city's seal (or its substitute) does not "stand for" Hill City; either can change without changing the other. Rather, the seal reminds us of the life of the city and condenses our scattered awarenesses of it, telling us all that what bears the seal is "official." What people make of that designation depends in part on what actually happens under its aegis. If the seal has its own life, it still doesn't exactly have a life of its own. What officials do can either strengthen it or weaken it. The interplay of people's recognition of the seal, their experience in association with it, may give the seal, insubstantial in itself, power and weight. The tax bill comes; if it is not paid, property will be seized. The building inspector must issue a permit; if not, a new building cannot be occupied. Decisions that would be, by themselves, arguable, become unarguable by becoming a part of what is, rather than matters subject to debate. "You can't fight city hall." Of course, the opposite can happen. "I saw a city work truck, and, sure enough, there were four guys standing there, watching one guy work." A plan with a pretentious title can be announced with fanfare, then left on a shelf to gather dust, its fading binding an apt metaphor for the misdirected effort itself. The impression of laziness, a feckless effort, or anything seen to go awry under the auspice of the seal weakens it.

Heraldry is not much of an art in the United States, so our occasional discussions of the city's seal and logo are all the more curious because they are so serious and so intense. Over a decade ago, the obvious incongruity of Ceres and the steam engine prompted the adoption, for public relations purposes, of the logo whose motif was "The City of Seven Hills," a classical reference and topographic characterization coined when the city was a tenth of its present area, and even then not particularly accurate. With the decline of classical education only a few of us recognized the reference to Rome enough to be bemused by dreams of a municipal empire. Round, executed in shades of green, the logo was a disk with seven angular squiggles on it, abstract representations of the alleged seven hills.

Done by a public relations firm, the logo served well enough, while drawing an occasional measure of underground aesthetic criticism: "Seven worms on a lily pad!" "Seven blips on a radar screen!"

As the city's big anniversary approached, a committee set itself the task of beautifying the highway approaches to the city, a worthy goal given the commercial clutter and decaying neighborhoods that make the approaches unquestionably ugly. With a view to finding some representation of the city that had something to do with the history of the city itself, they looked for a representation of either the Irishman who washed up here, started a ferry across the river, and married well, or his son, the real estate developer who got the city actually chartered back in the early days of the Republic. They couldn't find anything, so they settled for a full-length silhouette of a relative of the founders, in a top hat and with a cane. At least this new medallion was not rendered in the despised green, and it tried to refer to the actual history of the city itself instead of using the preposterous imperial slogan, but the unrecognizable individual in peculiarly old-fashioned dress didn't catch on. The Anniversary Committee did manage to come up with a recognizable, attractive representation of the city, a stylized view from across the river, the very river that had given birth to the ferry, then the landing, and then the settlement itself. The city manager, attentive to such matters when everyone else was otherwise occupied, began working on ways to adapt the anniversary symbol for eventual use as a new city logo.

He had mentioned it to me, and probably other council members, early on. It must have been the case that no one objected, because on his own (he described it all to us later) he went to the local and genuinely talented commercial artist who designed the anniversary emblem and got him to work on some modifications that would suit the design for municipal purposes. And he arranged a presentation for us, quietly and with no publicity, showing how the new symbol would be used on city stationery, vehicles, and so forth.

Isn't that a curious way to deal with something that would be so public, doing it so quietly and privately? Surely the first reaction of anyone considering a change in the city government's graphic symbol of itself would be to "go public," to invite suggestions, proposals, maybe have a contest with a lot of fanfare. But would such superficial, procedural democracy have democratic, civic results? If several usable designs were submitted, there would have to be winners and losers, and what is the point of more winners and losers if the city is a community that must, by definition, include both winners and losers? The anniversary emblem had been popular during the celebration; it had been widely reproduced on souvenirs, bumper stickers, banners, and the like. The anniversary itself had been popular, culminating in a giant parade and an unexpectedly moving "birthday party" in the city football stadium. A modified symbol of that series of events and impressions, inclusive and celebratory, would be inviting and positive, more so than any available alternative. Or at least one could argue that. Of course, that leaves a considerable burden in the hands of those who use the symbol; it must be used in ways that reinforce its expression of commonality, of a sense of the community that is broader than where we simply are and where we happen to have to do business. The identifying sign of the humdrum and prosaic tasks of the municipality can't be reduced to the humdrum. It's hard not to think that the city manager was right: procedural democracy at the inception of something may be desirable, but the real test is how the civic matter proceeds in the long run, in the contexts of the civic lines lived by all of us as private citizens.

Another funeral anecdote: D., then the Community Club president, called on the phone. "We're providing the pallbearers for Y.'s funeral. Would you be one of them?" Y. had been a club member, not long a resident of the city. Coming from New York City and a career in public relations, he seemed brash and "foreign." Retired, he had made strenuous efforts to create a social home for himself and his French Canadian wife by "participating in community affairs." But his cancer came quickly, and he died a painful death, refusing in his last weeks even to see visitors. The unspoken part of D.'s request (maybe, I never asked): "If you come, as a member of the council, it will be a little more public, not a semiprivate recitation of the funeral mass in an almost empty church." He did murmur something about not knowing "whether Y. knew a whole lot of people. . . ." The spoken answer to his unspoken question and whatever unspoken messages it brought along with it: "Sure. Glad to help out."

So I did. It was a cold, gray winter day with snow in the air and a thin cover of snow on the ground. The casket was heavy, and the ground was frozen. When spring came, his widow sold their house and moved back to Montreal.

Last funeral anecdote: a funeral over in the valley was, contrary to the usual journalistic practice, reported by the newspaper in complete detail. A self-proclaimed atheist carried out the first burial in his newly opened atheist cemetery, a patch of woods littered with debris and scrap machinery. The name of the deceased was not made public; he had been a prisoner in the state penitentiary and claimed no family. They carried his body to the grave in a plastic tarp and rolled it in with no ceremony at all. Then the hole was filled in. The mechanism of a human body had been discarded along with the other junk of the world. All of this was reported with careful attention to detail. The fellow who opened the cemetery picketed the church of our local TV evangelist some time ago; I think he was the one carrying a cross with a crucified frog on it. In any case, that effort to make death a purely private and mechanistic matter got more public attention than any formal funeral service in recent years.

Irony aside, the reciprocity of death and civic life seems obvious, and it seems to have been obvious for a long, long time. Over two millennia ago, the Athenian war leader Pericles addressed the survivors of Athenian soldiers killed early in the final war with Sparta. According to him, the merit of dying in the service of the city was so great that where a person had stood in society and what they did before the war no longer counted in shaping the public estimation of them: "Even . . . men of inferior character . . . wiped out their evil by their good. . . ." To be sure, as an effective interest-group politician, Pericles went on to point out that the funeral donated by the city of Athens was a direct monetary benefit to the surviving families who were thereby spared the rather large expense of the customary elaborate funeral. But he wouldn't have made the claim about civic sacrifice outweighing personal defects unless he thought his audience would believe it. And we can still understand what he meant; at our war memorials we come pretty close to demonstrating that we still believe about the same thing.

Yet no matter how constant the belief and practice, we, here and now, have a difficult time talking about it. We may know how to act about it—even if it took our city a generation to get around to commemorating our World War II dead—but we don't have much to say about it. The formulations from those philosophers of politics we say we follow, no one would dare repeat: Hobbes's, "No one can agree to their own death"; Locke's watered-down revision, "No one should just bear costs, they should get something out of it." No. They won't do at all. But we know what to do. It's not a part of what we say, it is a part of what we are.

A new memorial is built; people visit it. We dedicated our new memorials on the terrace. Afterward, many of those in the crowd walked up the steps, gathering in clusters at the separate landings where the different wars were commemorated, talking and reading the names. Occasionally, someone would reach out to touch one of the names cut deep in the stone.

I walked up, too, not lingering at any particular one. As I passed the Vietnam memorial, I noticed L. and his young son standing in front of it, looking at the names. L. had been severely wounded there; some of the scars still showed, and he could walk only with an obvious limp. I almost stopped to say something, then decided not to interrupt them and just walked on up, across the street, and over to the parking lot.

More often than those who are practiced users of words care to admit, what we do conveys more than what we're able to say. That crank over in the valley with his mechanical-parts cemetery is wrong. There are no facts apart from their contexts of meaning. When these meanings refer to human sacrifice for the community, then we are referring to the worth of human life.

If the city is ever to do anything, if we are ever to work together, we may still have things to learn from H.'s bees, but we won't do it the way the bees do it, compelled by biological makeup to assume preset roles and perform specific predetermined tasks. Our people, at least, are not bees or ants. They like to be persuaded, coaxed, and appealed to on their own terms and left alone a fair amount of time. What governance requires is their willingness. Willingness can neither be compelled nor created outright by slogans and propaganda. It can only be elicited, allowed to grow on its own, and the only thing our symbols can do in that process is provide a few meanings of very limited use and the suggestion of an unknowable range of possibilities. Willingness has to be nourished in a thousand small ways that frequently have little to do with what are usually defined as acts of governing, the vaunted "decision-making" that attracts so much naive attention. Willingness, the open, free consideration of some project, can't be encouraged much by material favors—they're too easy to corrupt, anyway. Willingness does require public recognition, even though that can be corrupted, too—applause, a medal, a certificate, a name on the Little League field scoreboard, or a list of names on a bronze plaque. It does require that those who exemplify the ultimate willingness—the willingness to risk one's life for the community—be recognized, especially those whose willingness costs them their lives. But when we try to express it in words, we sound silly, so no one complains about the uniform asininity of the speeches given at the dedications of war memorials, because everyone knows the words don't matter anyway. What counts are the names, carved deep in the stone.

Governing our city does not begin with the expression of an idea by somebody and the demonstration of the worth of that idea to large numbers of people. The governing that the city does—some important things, some less important things, some pointless things—begins with what is already being done. Politics grows out of the politicking that is already going on. The meaning of governing and politics grows out of our shared experience. After H.'s funeral people talked about it. Politics and governing are not separate from the rest of the city. No matter how insulated and self-absorbed some of the city-hall types are, they are still part of the world inhabited by the rest of the human race.

Public life and political activity do not transcend the ordinary world— they begin and end in it. There are enough politicos who want us to think otherwise. They would like everyone to believe that political position is extraordinary and can be the salvation of the community, not to mention the power-wielder himself. But it's not really so. At most, public life provides the officeholder with enough power to deceive himself. The power to be quoted in the newspaper, the power to squeeze personal favors out of city staff, the power to live it up with public money at conventions a couple of times a year—these powers and their like can create potent illusions in the minds of those who hold them.

Perhaps the power-wielders are so comfortable with these illusions because the alternative is so uncomfortable: if politics begins and ends in ordinary life, then it is condemned to the frustrations and failures of ordinary life. Most people eventually figure out that life is short and filled with effort. The human lot is not triumph: "Man dies, and he is unhappy." In its seals, plaques, monuments, and public commemorations, the city reflects this understanding that is so unfashionable to talk about. What the city can say in the face of this is, "We know." And because human efforts are nonetheless worth something, the community will try to pass them along. Thus, the city exerts its hold over us, not in words, not in the chatter of broadcast news or in the endless columns in the newspaper.

In such things as funerals, monuments, and commemorations, the city wordlessly *is*. In these and in its buildings and public works, the city gives us a possibility to fill the physical frame with a common life. Without the common life, they are "ghost towns" or, better yet, the "dead cities" of archaeologists.

Other cities have these symbols, too; perhaps that's an essential part of being a city. We insist on talking about cities in other terms, though, using the cramped, restricted vocabulary of textbooks and legal documents and bureaucrats, eternally fascinated by the rigid categories that let us reduce people to populations and work to dollar amounts. A city has population and wealth, but it is not these. Nor is it a concept nor a legally constituted corporation nor a political power structure.

Hill City doesn't exist until we allow ourselves to perceive it, to become conscious of it. And we become conscious of it only as we recognize that it can have meaning. It is not always the same for everyone, but there is still the possibility of sharing whatever meaning is there with someone: "Did you see the firemen?" "Yeah. I really choked up. It was nice of them to do that." "Yeah. Me too." The governing of Hill City is activity, but the activity isn't something that is complete in itself. It's messier than that. We are constantly under some impulse to express that activity with symbols. The symbols aren't neat and self-contained, either. They're not just simple, separate signs that serve as a convenient shorthand for simple, separate activities. They're more like a tangle of expressions— words, gestures, ceremonies, even simple courtesies, not to mention pictures, buildings, monuments—that may be tightly or loosely connected. But whatever they are and however they're connected, they are the medium through which we carry on what we manage to do. They permeate our doing and how we try to live with it. Any account of governance must be based on them. Our only choice is whether to be conscious of it, at least in part, or to sleepwalk through that which we presume to be directing.

THREE

Memory

The struggle of man against power is the struggle
of memory against forgetting.

—Milan Kundera, *The Book of Laughter and Forgetting*

It was gray and cold when the plane took off, but as we flew back toward the southeast the weather started to lighten, and by the time we were halfway over the mountains the afternoon sun had broken through the cloud cover. From our altitude (what had it been . . . twelve, fifteen thousand feet?) the black trunks of bare trees in the higher places couldn't be seen individually; they just gave a darker texture to the purplish brown of the fallen leaves and the gray of the rocks. But the valleys, the lower places, were different. Despite its being mid-November, they hadn't had any frost on them yet, and they were still green, almost glowing where the sunlight struck. We had left behind us the chopped, irregular mountains of the plateau and were flying over the long, even ridges of stretched-out mountains that run for miles in northeast-to-southwest folds. Beginning the approach to home, the pilot steered the plane lower over the great granite wrinkles. Still lower, slowly dropping, we stopped the chatter and jokes to stare out the window at the landscape displayed before us.

The sun, bright and clear and low in the southwest, seemed to be spilling a gold and emerald honey of light down the troughs of the valleys, filling them from the bottoms with translucent greens and yellows in a last hypnotizing reminder of the prodigality of summer. Only the trees and bushes with leaves still on them caught the light; the black branches of the ridgetops generated their own contrasting gloom. Reversing the usual order, the high places were dim and cool, the valleys bright and inviting. Visible now in detail, individual farms with their barns, houses, and fence-lines were transfigured; they were no longer muddy, economically doubtful enterprises, but freshly discovered evidence that beauty and use can mingle, that the daily round can embody perfection, if only for a moment.

I imagined that mountains, streams, houses, people, everything, could be preserved in some miraculous amber that might stretch the moment out forever.

No one spoke. We just stared out the starboard windows, listening to the whine of the engines and looking up the long, straight valleys toward the sun. It was as if we were being reassured that the silliness and showmanship and toil of the weekend had been worth it. Then, gradually, gently, the moment lost its hold. How long had it lasted, five, seven minutes? Neither. It was both an instant and an eternity. The spell softened and gracefully broke: "Looks like somethin' out of National Geographic!" "Yeah!"

The southern mountains, alternately enticing and violent—airy and flirtatious in spring, awesomely fecund in summer, but also capable of spawning devastating floods, overwhelming storms, and man-killing cold. It is easier to understand them in winter, when the leaves are gone and the hard geometry of the granite shows on the knobs and cliff faces and in the clefts of the streams. Like that trip to the Smoky Mountains, when three of us left Atlanta in late fall sunshine and arrived in the middle of the first mountain snowstorm of the season. There wasn't much prospect of backpacking in three days the projected thirty miles that we had worked out on the map. The temperature dropped to zero that night, freezing the water in the canteens and the eggs in their shells, leaving Scotch whiskey as our principal unfrozen refreshment. The next morning, W., with his Fuji stick, led the way up the ridge through the dry, deep snow—nothing was moving but us and a startled grouse or two. The sky was bright blue, the mountains surprisingly angular and bony. Until that trip, I had only seen the Smokies in summer, when the tree leaves hid their ruggedness, softening their harsh topography.

The snow was nearly hip deep at the top of the first ridge, so we turned around, retraced our steps, and packed out along the river. Shallow and fast, it hadn't frozen yet. Its water looked black next to the snow-covered banks, but when we stopped to look it was actually clear, showing each stone on the bottom. Spray had frozen on the mossy rocks sticking up above the surface of the dark, fast-moving water, and where the sunlight struck the rocks there was another gift of the mountains: encased in frozen spray, the moss on the round, worn rocks reflected deep green rays of light, wreathed with rays of pure white light from the surrounding lace of ice. First one was revealed, then more as the sunlight struck them, a lavish display of jeweled brilliance in the barren forest. I stopped to stare, amazed at seeing this in a landscape of snow, naked trees, and dull rock, reminded of how often we miss the possibilities that lie dormant in what is actually before us. The others marched on heedlessly, content with whatever private visions were flickering across their minds. I had to jog to catch up. The revelation was mine alone.

But the flight home from the municipal award competition was different. We had worked together for the entire weekend and had all shared the anxiety and enthusiasm leading up to the final presentation before the jury. E. had displayed a talent for leadership that bordered on genius and had gotten a lot of willing, even intelligent help. The final presentation went better than we had dared to hope. The point of our presentation was not to try for a hard sell with flashy civic imagery, but instead to call attention to the projects themselves by bringing the "project people"—the leaders, the workers, and the beneficiaries themselves, not political figures—to the national meeting. And of all these project people, J. had had the greatest impact, giving her soft, slow reply to one judge's cocky question. R. would have been the one expected to make the response—the proper, correctly attired, white southern lady with the authoritative air. But instead of responding with a barrage of statistics to the question about her poverty counseling program, she just fixed a calm, level stare at the judge, said, "I think you want to hear from J.," and stepped back from the microphone. J., a shy, heavy, pretty black woman, spoke in a low, heavily accented voice, holding her head down, stopping every once in a while to look up directly, as if to see that the judge understood. She explained that the program had helped her find heated housing and get a loan, which she had successfully paid back. When "her baby" was old enough for Head Start, J. said, she was going to go back and finish high school so that she could get a good job and—she ended with a note of triumph in her voice— "my children won't grow up on welfare."

The entire room was silent. The judge who had asked the question looked vaguely sheepish, and a couple of other judges seemed visibly delighted at his having gotten a penetrating answer to an almost flippant question. The atmosphere brightened, and the rest of the questions were easy—a lot of queries about the details of C.'s really incredible low-income homeowner program. Close to the end, when it looked like the water-quality volunteers weren't going to get a question, G. barged up, announced that she hadn't come this far to say nothing, and answered a question she thought they should have asked. When it was over, we were applauded; none of the others had been, so we were all elated. People congratulated J. again and again, and it all seemed worth it—sticking our little embroidered emblems on other people's lapels, running an almost nonstop hospitality suite, overseeing all the details of shipping and setting up the display—so that for just one euphoric moment we could feel that we had something worth saying on behalf of the whole city, that we had said it, and that everyone else there had believed it.

The dazzling, late-afternoon vision from the airplane seemed a coda to all that had gone before, reducing us to silence. As we left the mountains the plane banked over Valley City, then east toward Hill City, fifty miles away. Valley City was half our age, but had twice our population. After a little prompting (flying charter has its advantages), the pilot announced we were passing over Valley City, a "relatively well known suburb of Hill City," and everyone cheered. The pilot took us back to the northwest to bring the plane around town so the landing approach would be directly over the center of the city. But things still didn't look familiar. Huge funnels of smoke, scattered all over town, were rising in the clear autumn air, making it look as if the city were burning. Of course, there was the usual flash of inner alarm—a house? my house?—but it was just people burning leaves, nothing more. The slight, even breeze and the clear air kept the huge plumes of smoke intact, making home look strange and foreign. Someone, in a pointless imitation of W.C. Fields, drawled, "Ahaaa. The campfires of Jenghiz Khan, stretching to the horizon." The street pattern flashed by underneath, lower, faster, past the window, then the Metroliner's wheels bumped and screeched as it finally touched down. The local television station's news crew was waiting for us at the terminal gate. That was good—prompt coverage while everyone was still excited. Maybe some of the enthusiasm would come through on television. There would be no chance to explain any of it at length, so that people would come close to understanding, but still the hope remained that somehow it could all get across. . . . It was also nice to get a little personal publicity. There was some discussion on the plane about who would get off first. E. straightened his tie; A. got out a magnetized sign of the city logo to slap onto the side of the plane, designating it "Hill City One" for the cameras. The blue shadows of evening were stretching across the runways and open spaces of the airport. There was a little horsing around, some talk for the camera, then on to our own homes—familiar, settled, home at last.

What did we accomplish and what "history," if any, would there be of what we had tried to do? The twenty of us who had gone talked about it for weeks afterward, but our exhilaration was hard to explain to those who hadn't been there. Telling how it had been in front of the jury, how we could feel everyone pulling for us—there was no sense trying to convey it. We could only tell them we were excited, hope they'd get interested in some way, and let it go at that. It would be nice if they could be convinced to look at what's around them, what's already there, with fresh appreciation—no, bad idea. There was no sense in trying to convince them that a lot of what they see each day and take for granted, a lot of what they dismiss as "ordinary," or assume that "everyone knows" about them, are really very noteworthy things—triumphs of the human spirit, evidences of God's grace that they've been too blind to see. Nor would there ever be a public account of all the costs despite the careful attention to fund-raising and care of the money and so on. For example, E. found out that an employee of his had made a major foul-up and lost his small business a sizable account, all because E. had gone to the conference and, as a result, had not devoted himself wholly to his private affairs. A last piece of evidence: A., after the city government had received a patently stupid request for city money from people whose "community standing" would have led a naive person to expect them to propose something practical and sensible, muttered under his breath, "This . . . stuff . . . I wish more people could have been at that conference, to see this city at its best."

After a couple of months the excitement died down, and we just kept waiting to hear whether or not we had won the award. If someone were to presume to write a "history" of that effort (names, dates, places, and all), it could only be rendered in terms of whether we had actually won the award for the first time, and perhaps how that was commemorated. What it had meant to us—the event itself and the significance of the plane ride back—would be ignored. Yet those of us who saw them as demonstrations of public possibility will remember them, holding that memory as a benchmark for what is possible, reminding ourselves of what can be worthwhile—and remembering the costs to E. of getting caught up in it. But if those embedded memories, the recollections of what it was "like," shape what we do later in indirect and unknown ways, what would be the good of a "history" of what happened? What would be the good of a factual, "objective" account, unclouded by concerns about meaning? The various printed versions of the city's history mostly gather dust on library shelves, occasionally raided for trivia by high-school term-paper writers and roving genealogists.

In contrast to the formal "histories" on the shelves, people walk around the city with their own memories of living here. These memories are the images and stories of the past that guide the perceptions of these real, live people. Anyone who presumes to guide Hill City must know its history, and to know its history, it is necessary to have some sense of these lived histories that are walking around in each of us. They are the repositories that people have of what is real, of what Hill City is.

There are memories of small things, like this one from a local businessman, looking with me at a section of street in a decaying neighborhood that seemed so worn that I thought it must have been there forever: "When I was a boy that street was just a sand track, and I used to ride my pony down there as fast as we could go. Boy, I could make her fly!" And there are deeper, more troubling memories, too. From a retired and embittered old man who had been the "first black" on a number of things, including city council, recalled in his semidarkened room: "A white woman, any white woman, was referred to as 'Mrs.' or 'Miss.' No black woman was ever anything but plain Ann Smith." It had been the newspaper's psychological enforcement of segregation that had made the biggest impression on him forty years before, when he was a young man, and the memory still possessed his thoughts. He recounted vividly the newspaper's account of *Miss* Trixie X.'s arrest for prostitution; in that same edition the story reporting the earning of master's degrees in education by black schoolteachers carefully omitted any "Miss" or "Mrs." before the names. He was old, sensing the steady approach of death, and that was his essential memory of the city, the baseline from which he saw his own later achievements and recognitions as nothing.

Another memory of another person: at a national conference of municipal officials—in Denver, far from home and familiar faces—I was wandering around at the first evening's cocktail reception when a distinguished, intelligent-looking gentleman—trim build, well dressed in a gray suit that complemented his silver hair and moustache—stopped to stare at my delegate badge. It wasn't my name but the city's name that had so caught his attention. It had triggered some powerful memories (or maybe nostalgia), and with a wistful, completely unguarded sigh in his voice he murmured, "Tell me, is 'Louise's' still there?" Louise's had been the best known of the brothels of the city's once-famous red-light district, a destination of recreation for thousands of GI's during World War II, and the man in front of me was obviously one of the more satisfied customers. The present condition of "the street" and the small size of the houses on it make it hard to credit the aura of sophistication and opulence that some attach to "the district" of yore, but someone or something had made a lasting impression on him. I made the only answer I could: "No, sir. I'm sorry, but it's long gone." We chatted amiably for a few minutes, and he sort of drifted off, serene, his mind fifteen hundred miles and thirty-five years away.

But memory is not purely personal and accidental; it is, after all, memory of something, and sometimes we even cultivate that memory, anticipating it and inviting others to join in. Like the time E. and I decided after a meeting to drive down to the riverfront and see how much further the water had risen. To the west of us, the rain in the mountains had been both heavy and extensive—a rare combination of circumstances that had its most striking effects on areas like ours, in the lower portions of the watersheds, where the water was rising into unprecedented floods. My older son and I had gone down the evening before, just as the river topped flood stage, but it hadn't been very dramatic—just a slightly ominous tinge of excitement in the air, since most people had heard the news that the water was rising fast and could be expected to keep on rising. At the official flood stage, the river is out of its banks, but still so far down in what is almost a canyon that an official flood doesn't necessarily look like much. So, there hadn't been much for us to wonder at. We crossed the viaduct, parked the car, and watched a little. Back over on the city side we could see the water rising in one of the river-bottom areas that was used as a parking lot, and we watched the level of the water move up the wheels of the handful of vehicles that had evidently been left for the time being to the mercies of the oncoming flood. The various electric lights in the bottom reflected out onto the surface of the main channel of the river, where the eddies and swirls were building up and beginning to seem rough and threatening, but that was all. We watched awhile, then went back home.

But the second night, when E. and I went down after the meeting, it was easy to tell that something quite out of the ordinary was going on. The flood by now had knocked out some key power lines in its relentless rise, and on the avenue, after we passed the women's college, all the lights were out—house lights, street lights, traffic lights—leaving everything in an unaccustomed and complete darkness, giving the almost empty street a strangely primitive air. There were a few other cars, but not many, and their headlights seemed unusually garish and bright, the only illumination in the urban gloom.

When we got down to the viaduct and riverfront area we found that the firemen had blocked the viaduct and set up floodlights on it, running them by portable generators. We walked past them and down to the streets that usually ran downhill toward the river, but where the water was now creeping steadily uphill. Yellow tape marked the police lines intended to hold spectators well back from the water, but the crowds were gone as well as most of the police, so we ducked under the tape and walked down toward the dark, advancing water, listening to it hiss and burble around the buildings and walls, the telephone poles, the lampposts, and the trees.

Then we went back over to the viaduct where the floodlights were glaring back in our eyes, obscuring the rescue and fire trucks that were part of the waiting as the water rose up the piers of the viaduct, almost up to the tops of the arches that supported each span. Alongside, the first floors of the old warehouses flanking the part of the viaduct that crossed over the bottomland were completely under water. Huge clouds of steam, lit up by the floodlights, were billowing out of one of the buildings, making things even more weird and mysterious. We did not know that large amounts of carbide had been stored in one old building and that the water had finally reached it. We would have stayed to watch (from a distance, of course) if we had known that the acetylene gas being generated by the water and the carbide was accumulating and would explode in ten minutes. In the next day's paper there was a picture of the building burning, flames shooting out of the windows and from the roof, completely surrounded by flood waters and left to burn itself out, a strange composite image of simultaneous destruction by both fire and water.

We had also run into K., with his son, doing the same thing we were doing: marking the extent of the flood, making a conscious effort to establish a memory of the time of the remarkable flood of '85. And by doing it with someone, especially K. and I having taken our sons with us, we were silently saying, "Remember this. Remember the darkness and the wash of the river on what we thought were things destined to be forever high and dry. Remember the muddy smell of the river and those on guard in the gloom, lighting the night in an unaccustomed way, resuming the old, taken-for-granted task of the night watch. Remember us doing this, and sometime with your son, you'll do something like this in turn and remember me. . . ."

If there is anything that will be a "history" of the flood, it will note that it had been the highest since 1796, that the city utilities alone suffered $5 million in damage, that no one was killed. But what may never be put down is the cluster of varied perceptions and memories, somehow tied together by the events themselves and by the stories about the flood: "We were on top of the bank building and watched it all from there. We saw the chemical canisters float past and the roof of that house, too." Or: "I'll be forever getting the mud and the smell out. You don't have *any idea* what water can do *inside* a house." Most curious of all, the calendar, the events of that season, become measured in terms of the flood. Presumably given precision and objectivity by being numbered, our calendar turns out to be quite relative, anchored by events like the flood: "Lessee, the flood was on election day so that would make it early in November, and it was a couple of weeks after the flood that X. happened, so that makes it the middle of November. . . ." At least for us, the time of something like the flood is a different kind of time, a time that we take pains to mark out from other kinds of time, to remember specifically. Our civic time is not a continuum. It is not marked off in equal parts for an eternal procession of equal moments. It is instead an uneven accumulation of significances, greater or lesser as the case may be, a mosaic of perceptions that may cohere or may not.

I am reminded of the one time that I couldn't resist the urge to ask the staff about someone else's business. In addition to being in bad taste, asking about matters that are out of your hands, settled, or won't come before the council, does impose obligations. It's better to let staff come to you with an offer of tempting, irrelevant pieces of gossip; that's a smaller obligation, and it puts the informant in the position of being the one who either can't control himself or is seeking to stay in your good graces. But in this case, the outcome was so far removed from what I had expected that I broke the rules and asked anyway.

The bridge replacement had already been delayed twice, and we were in the bad graces of the state highway department for asking for design changes, engaging in politicking, and taking part in the general fiddling around that goes with trying to act outside the established procedures. So until this pair—sister and brother—brought it up again, we had thought the question of the replacement was finally settled. The sister called me, courteous to the point of being ingratiating, but still determined—very determined, as it turned out.

Not that very much was required of me; all I had to do was assure her that appearing before the Public Works Committee was the correct step and promise her that I would be there to inform myself about the entire business. After all, the highway department enjoys being high-handed occasionally, so a smart-aleckiness aimed at them from time to time is satisfying, if mildly disruptive. If the highway engineers were planning on moving more dirt than was absolutely necessary, and doing it in a year when construction funds were in short supply, it would be fun to catch them out.

So sister and brother came. They were neat and well groomed in their appearance; their clothes were just a little casual, not the usual "downtown" attire. It was almost country dress—he shod in what seemed to be new brown walking shoes with crepe soles, she in espadrilles—a polite, tacit statement that they didn't feel the need to dress for city hall to assert their standing as people to be taken seriously. After all, they were scions of a well-known local family that was prominent in commerce. Both had gray hair and were cherubic looking—children gently aged before life had a chance to ravage them much. She was intent; he was distracted and fretful.

Though the embankment along their property was scheduled to be cut back only a few feet, even that minimal displacement would take two large, old oaks growing next to the white board fence that framed their gracious mansion. The loss wouldn't have been a disaster, exactly, but it would have diminished the spacious, shaded yard of the place where they had grown up and still lived. They had brought a large map with them that located and described every tree and large shrub on the front part of the property, with those that would be taken specially marked. A landscape architect had come with them, mostly to shake his head in sorrow as far as this particular meeting was concerned, since as a practical matter he had no alternative to offer. The most modest widening of the present roadbed would take the trees.

With the trees gone, the property would be a little devalued and a little . . . what? nude? But for them, it seemed deeper and more complicated than a regard for greenery or a few dollars or a detached love of beauty. It would be a genuine personal loss for the huge oak sentinels to go, a diminishing of their understanding of themselves, not reducible to so many board feet of lumber or seven months of shade each year. Behind their plea for the trees lay more—an idyllic childhood, in fact or fancy: long summer afternoons spent in the shade listening to the drone of locusts and, from the kitchen, the clatter and the low burble of servants' voices; girls arriving in proper dresses for an ice cream party; boys uncomfortable in stiff collars and spoiling for more activity than was planned or allowed; their father, not as he had become—more a memory than a person, a pale wraith no longer active, waiting for the end—but in his prime, known and vigorous. . . .

Still, we thought they were asking for something they couldn't get. We considered the business settled: six years before we had gotten the project scaled-down from four lanes to two and had scuttled plans for an entirely new roadbed that would really have damaged the property. They seemed genuinely surprised to hear about that piece of highway history; either they had never known or they had completely forgotten about it. The rural bridge in its no-longer-rural setting was itself a continuing sore spot with the driving public who were using it in urban volumes. It was on a section of narrow, winding road that betrayed its origins, with large, picturesque sycamores and oaks on either side and no shoulders or proper drains. Being wooden made the bridge bad enough in the public perception, but what scared nearly everyone was the way the planks in the flooring would work themselves loose and make an alarming racket when cars and trucks went over. The shaded, eastern approach was uphill in addition to being narrow, with a tendency to get icy in winter. At the state's statutorily required location hearing, two men from the neighborhood recounted vivid stories of giving first aid and calling ambulances when cars would lose traction, slide off the road, and crash into the picturesque trees.

The highway engineers had assured us long ago that the old bridge was structurally safe, and they were continually distressed that most people didn't believe them. They never quite grasped that it's hard to believe that a wooden bridge over one hundred years old that sounds like it's coming apart as you drive over it can be perfectly safe. So the engineers had gotten themselves distressed, and they became sentimental. The sunburned guys in khaki work pants and muddy boots who were ready to redo creation with dynamite and bulldozers were sentimental about what they could appreciate, but that was lost on the insensitive, ignorant herd. They were caught up with what they saw as their history: the reputation of their profession and its authority and credit with the public. It was the last Fink truss bridge in actual use! Built elsewhere and so reliable that it could be hauled in (this one from California, they said) and just dropped into place over the railroad cut, plop, nothing to it, for the public to use in complete safety! The newspaper published a couple of stories about the remarkable bridge. Proposals to preserve it were floated—could it be set up in a park as part of a technological museum, so people wouldn't forget? All this from supposedly practical, utilitarian engineers. But they were not practical engineers any longer—now they were romantic heroes imposing order on wilderness and demanding recognition of their daring and skill.

Everyone involved had slogged along. Romantic or not, the old bridge would be replaced and its approaches would be straightened out. An affordable, comparatively modest new bridge was installed, not a four-lane testament to the potency of contemporary construction techniques, but just a replacement of the bridge and its approaches. One older couple of modest means was required to give up a large part of their already small front yard. There was concern for them—compassion does surface from time to time—and some adjusting. This had all gone on, episode after episode, and here they were, sister and brother, with a new version, a new history of something we thought was settled.

I tried to be nice while wondering what earthly use it was to resurrect the whole thing again. I suggested some possible actions. Maybe (but not likely, I was sure) there was a way to accommodate them. After all, the highway department does over-engineer things, but S. was preemptory. "We've done all this, and you're asking us to stop the project?" He was almost sarcastic, but S. did put an edge on things sometimes; it was probably another old score to settle.

But that had been all of it for me this time around. I sat at the meeting, made sure they got a hearing, and figured that was going to be that. The sister had a guest column on the paper's editorial page about highways and trees, but I didn't pay a lot of attention. Then one day I saw her come barreling out of our street in her hatchback, hauling something with the back open and using our street to dogleg around the stoplight up at the main intersection. I had no chance to respond to her smile and wave. It did seem an inordinately cheerful gesture coming from someone who had recently lost a major battle.

The reason she was so cheerful was that she hadn't lost. I found out about it later, when as a matter of administrative routine I received a copy of the relevant correspondence in a council packet: it announced, with no explanation, that the matter had been resolved to the satisfaction of all, and that the trees would not be cut.

How could that have happened when the trees were smack on the edge of the old roadcut and it was impossible to improve that part of the road without taking the trees? So, I violated the rules; I asked the staff for information I didn't need, on the street outside City Hall after a night meeting. The air was brisk, but I was able to get B. to stop for a few minutes. I asked, and a big smile cracked across his face: "Oh, hell! She wrote to the congressman, both U.S. senators, and the governor. What finally happened was that one of the engineers came to see her and told her that he was the best she was going to get!"

He stopped like that was the end of the story, so I had to reiterate: "But what happened?" "Oh. We just won't take the work that far this time. Have to go through the whole thing later when we do the rest of it."

"Well I'll be damned." They had gotten what they wanted, at least temporarily.

We are not quite the rational, goal-centered doers that we like to imagine we are. True, we have projects from time to time, and in particularly lucid moments we rationally construct what might be defensively described as reasonable means of bringing them about. But these are mere episodes or, better, occasional superstructures built on foundations that we somehow think it's intelligent to pretend aren't there. It's as if in going fishing I assumed that the ocean and the bays and inlets were simply the sum of the fish in them and nothing else, forgetting the water, the vast currents, the plankton, the diatoms, and whatever other bugs biologists have found there, the confluences of things and the myriad relations without which the flounder and croaker and bluefish couldn't exist and without which I could not conceive of going out. The encompassing context, not the project, is the starting point, and not just the natural context, but the human context, too. Before going, I presume fish that can be eaten, fire to cook them, boats, frying pans, and all. The isolation of "going fishing" is no starting point at all, it is the end; it is an audacious act of selective stupidity, to take for granted that which cannot be taken for granted, a stunt to let me concentrate on getting more fish without regard for the consequences.

Our projects don't bring us to their contexts. They give us instead a useful, if illusory, freedom from context that lets us attend to the object of our heart's desire and our mind's cunning. Anything is easier to pursue if we imagine it exists in isolation, though while we pursue it we tempt something in the environment to which we are not attending, something that will catch up on us while we are ignoring it. Assume a plan of action for which I need help: Primus has something to offer, so with him I need to be careful, offer something in return, and enlist him when the time is ripe. Secundus is probably a barrier; I will have to either beat him or avoid him. But Tertia (note how it starts to break down)—Tertia, hmmm. She might well be a diversion to a different project entirely. . . . How to choose? An entirely different project might be easier, unless Secundus remembers the time when . . . (Ha. Clever rascal, aren't you? Almost fell into the trap and then saw it coming at the last minute. Secundus would remember the time when . . . and he would be set in cement.) We're remembering, always remembering; there's no thinking forward without thinking back at the same time, dragging the baggage of the past along. What we imagine is inconceivable without what we remember. Without both past and future, we have no sense of time. If we have no sense of time we can make no judgments; that is, we cannot decide to do this now. "Well, I don't think I can support him next election. Maybe he's voted right, but he did support R. for governor." "A lot of people did. That was no test. Where did he stand on L.?" "Uhn. Maybe you're right." Or again: "You may not remember me, but I voted for you, and I'd like . . ."

U. has said that "if everyone who says they voted for me really did vote for me, I would have gotten 120 percent of the vote." Even someone who doesn't live in the district and couldn't have voted for you if his life depended on it may still use exactly the same words: "You may not re-member me, but . . ." By saying that, by establishing even an illusory memory of a nonexistent past, it becomes possible to plausibly address the future. Not in general, but personally. By establishing a personal memory to a benchmark public event (the election) it becomes possible to evoke a bond that obliges me to respond: "Yes, tell me your name again?" Of course, not everyone says it that way, maybe it's just those who feel the strongest need for a personal tie. Some seem to recognize an official role that they can tap into without evoking personal memory, especially if there's been some media publicity about something. For example: "R. called before you got home. He said that if you wanted to use it, you might be interested in knowing that two of the channels on the upper tier aren't coming in either." I had been publicly a little critical of the cablevision franchisee's performance while most of the rest of the council had been publicly apologetic for the service, even though there was some discontent with it. And so a context had been established.

There are more variations, but the theme is the same: I remember, you should remember (the moral imperative, bound to identity and memory). What is about to be asked (or offered) is in harmony with what our common memory says *is*. There is no separation of "is" and "ought." In these discourses, each defines the other.

These are not just vague, personal matters—they become an integral part of how city hall works. T., S., and I, in a conversation about the new city council chamber and how council meetings should be run, recalling a turbulent meeting of some time past: "I thought we were gonna have a fight. Right there. He looked like he was headed right over the bench!" "I don't want anything like that ever to happen again!" The two of them shared the same reaction, and it was still clear and vivid for them, even though it had happened seven years earlier. It was an event I had forgotten, even though I had been at the center of it. Curious that it impressed them so much more than it did me. After all, I was the one that the guy had headed for; maybe I had been the only one to see his face clearly and understand that he was excited, but not violent. He was a tall, rangy man, seemed to be used to outdoor work, and had come to complain about estimates (or was it the actual bill? I forget) of some water service connections the city had made at his house. So, he had just headed for the bench shouting and waving his papers, taking long strides that brought him from the pewlike seats to the high-fronted bench in an instant. All he had wanted was for someone to look at some figures on the papers he was waving about; I hadn't thought anything more about it after it was over.

But S. and T. had remained convinced that he was going to take a swing at somebody, and that had shaped their basic sense of what should and should not happen at council meetings. It had happened in the old council chamber, a high-ceilinged, windowless room that was wider than it was long, giving a sense of the audience being crammed up against the bench. The place had a forbidding atmosphere, and before the incident that alarmed S. and T. so much occurred, we had taken out the old-fashioned courtroom railing that had served as a barrier between the audience, the council bench, and the press and staff tables. Some regarded this as a radically populist step. With no proper restraint between council and the frenzied masses, there was no telling what sort of outrages might be perpetrated, or so they seemed to think. The supposed wild man who stormed the bench had been proof enough for them, if not for me.

Did I miss something? He had objected specifically to some stated costs for valves and pipe for his connection to city water service and, in the middle of a discussion about water service costs, had just jumped up and strode to the bench, calling for attention and shoving the papers at me. Abrupt and loud, yes, but terrifying?

Whatever the case, it no longer matters. The memories of the event are more important than any factual account that might be considered a "history" of it. S.'s impression was strong enough to make him determined to arrange things differently in the new chamber, and he used his position on the Building Committee to make sure that the architect for the new council chamber came up with a design that would soothe and muffle. In the new arrangements, all the seating is offset; no one faces anyone else directly. Everyone is seated, including those who address the council; they must come forward, and be seated again at a little table. You can't address the council standing on your own two feet. There is blue, deep-pile carpeting—no audible footsteps, not like the echoing floor of the old room that caught and emphasized the determined tread of someone coming forward or the stamp of angry feet storming out. The lighting is soft and indirect. The long, blue-gray curtain behind the council bench only seems to be in one piece; at each chair there's a hidden gap in the curtain marked at floor level by reflective orange tape. If an occasion were to call for it, in the new chamber all a council member need do is spin around in his swivel chair, take one step through the gap in the curtain, and—poof!—disappear. S. was very concerned about security, but in the years since there has been no occasion to use the elaborate arrangements.

Like archaic cephalopods dragging their misshapen shells across the floor of a primordial sea, we carry with us our personal histories, each with its own strange form, at once burdens and refuges, the definitions of our lives. Whatever the great events around them—the birth and death of oceans, the rise and fall of continents—they still have their own stubborn presence. Like B., who at the appropriate time in a sufficiently relaxed conversation could announce that he was "one of the few people who thoroughly enjoyed World War II." He intended only a mild shock, for he was a sensitive man as well as an intelligent and sophisticated one. Maybe he wanted to make the point that "every cloud has a silver lining," or maybe it was just his sense of humor at work. But for him, getting attached to the RAF and flying intelligence missions over the Nazi-occupied Balkans had been a refuge from a disintegrating marriage and a failing business. The global, political cataclysm that brought the Holocaust, atomic bombs, and millions of dead had brought him challenge, excitement, relief, and a store of fascinating anecdotes. But the point was clear enough—personal histories may run alongside "history," but they are separate from it.

"History," whatever it is and whoever keeps track of its precise course (it does have a precise course, doesn't it?), is something other than our own lives. Hill City has no definitive, collective history that I can find. Certainly there is no single account, no place where there are final renditions of what "really happened." What happens here, and what it means for each of us, is captured in our memories. Plural: memories. The unity of "what happened" lies in the events themselves. If someone were to write a history (if that is not a dead ambition, not to mention whether or not anyone would take the time to read it if there were such a history), they would have to start and finish in the memories of those who were here.

FOUR

•

Context

The principle by which the cyclist keeps his balance
is not generally known.

—Michael Polanyi, *Personal Knowledge*

No one ever said anything about there being an architecture of public finance, but there it was, plain as day and just waiting to be recognized. Maybe it took actually going into the building, really calling on someone at the Federal Reserve to see it fully, instead of just driving past one more big marble building while concentrating on the frenzied Washington traffic. Three and a half hours before, we had piled into the van donated for the trip by a Hill City motel owner and made the drive to the nation's capital in high spirits, cracking jokes and anticipating the pleasant occasion to come. And so "the Fed" loomed before us, no longer just one of the gracefully aging piles of stone along the Mall, but the focus of our excursion, opening a new awareness.

The building was done in a stern, simple, neo-Roman style. Made of white and gray marble and set back from the berserk river of automobiles on Constitution Avenue, it looked remote from the petty concerns of the rushing masses. Both building and setting were evocative of the Mediterranean world or whatever vision of time and space had fired the imagination of the architect who got the contract and conceived of it all. The Republic's citadel of money and banking, among the other grandiose buildings along the north side of the Mall, had its own air of serenity and imperial *gravitas.*

Just this one time, we would be significant visitors to this grand and remote home of the national commitment to money and banking. Proof of our importance for a day, we didn't have to prospect the street for a parking place, find it, walk to the building, clamber up the steps, and then go through a mere door. Following the previously given directions, we zipped around to the side, drove through the open gate in the great iron fence, and headed down a dip to the semiconcealed underground parking garage.

It was flattering, but a little disconcerting. The austerely classical environment changed abruptly: What was this glass and aluminum, flat-topped security booth, complete with a bored, uniformed guard? It struck a more . . . what? Germanic note? Was it a little Checkpoint Charlie at some secret border we were only now privileged to glimpse? This guard booth, amid the anachronistic grandeur of the building, struck the others as odd, too: "A Redi-Teller! Anyone need to get some cash?" "Don't tell 'em I'm here. I think I'm overdrawn!"

There were more chuckles and murmurs as the guard lazily waved us through. We whisked down the ramp and into the space under the building. There was no marble there; now it was concrete, structural steel, galvanized duct-work, and painted directional signs. But our initial impression of elegance came back when we got into the elevator; it was not lined with brushed aluminum, plastic, or mirrors, but with soft, brown Leatherette. The waist-high handhold was a small brass rail that ran around the interior, more the ambience of a sedan chair than a functionally necessary electric hoist. No more smart-alecky remarks about cashing or bouncing checks, just a few "Mmmms" and "Ahhhs."

At the appointed floor, we emerged like butterflies from a single giant cocoon and flocked down the hallway behind our guide. Our reason for being there was to publicize the striking of a silver medal to commemorate our city's most notable and politically powerful native son. During his tenure in the United States Senate, he had been a leading light in the creation of the regulatory agency we were visiting, and we, a delegation from his hometown, had come to present the board's chairman with one of the medals. But before the presentation, they led us to the shrine erected to the joint memory of our man and the president of the United States who was his colaborer in the vineyards of twentieth-century national financial policy. Like an aisle chapel in a cathedral, it was illuminated by sunlight streaming in the windows, and it was (again) mostly marble. There was a gracious, imposing widening at the end of the corridor, and bas-relief busts of the senator and the president, each with the appropriate marble commemorative tablets, dominated the walls on either side. Tastefully arranged sprays of flowers lent a splash of color to the pristine setting, all of it bathed in the natural brilliance of daylight.

We stood for a moment in reverential silence. No one seemed to think that we ought to do anything like kneel or say a prayer, so we just stood, pilgrims awed by this unexpected shrine to Historical Significance. Gradually, members of the group started straggling individually back down the corridor to the meeting room where we would make the presentation. There the style changed again. We were struck once more, but not by classic dignity, government-issue security booths, or chapels to mammon. This time it was an out-sized evocation of feudal puissance.

This was the formal meeting room of the Board of Governors, done in the style of a French château's banquet hall: chandelier, fireplaces at each end, and a great table. The table was like the one that the lord of the manor and his men must have gathered round to moot the pressing questions of the day: "Ought we send anyone to the current crusade?" "Has subinfeudation gotten out of hand?" "Do any upstart clergy bear watching?" But it wasn't quite like that. The fireplaces were big enough to barbecue a whole steer each; the table was the size of a small skating rink; the chandelier could have accommodated Douglas Fairbanks and two stuntmen, had they been directed to swing from one side of the room to the other. No, it wasn't a French baronial hall; it was just done in that style to a different, gargantuan scale—Hollywood baronial.

We fanned out into the expanse of the room, drinking in this latest installment of grandeur, then gratefully accepted the invitation to be seated at the table. At each place lay a heavy, slightly worn binder—quietly upscale, like wearing an expensive shirt with a barely frayed collar—holding the inevitable yellow legal pad, with a ballpoint pen alongside and an ashtray with a book of matches. The matchbook covers had a nice design. They were simple, white covers marked with the seal of the Fed in gold: eagle rampant with a shield of the United States, olive branch and oak leaves below, ringed by the words, "Board of Governors of the Federal Reserve System." As we found our ways to our places, I managed to pocket three of the matchbooks. On later examination of one, I found at the small end, in tiny letters, the notice, "Made in Canada."

Next to me, B. found his seat and, as we waited for what would be a pleasant ceremony with the chairman, opened one of the folders to see what notes might still be there, clues to what went through the minds of the governors as they played out their roles as economic Fates, spinning and cutting off. He found no numbers or written reminders, no lists of winners and losers in the metamorphosis of interest rates, no sketched maps of oil sheikhdoms. He did find one small cartoon, passably executed, of the well-known bald head of the chairman as seen from directly above. A pigeon's-eye view? The pad at my place was completely empty.

The chairman came in, greeted us, and gave a quite well prepared little talk on our native son's role in national financial policy. The commemorative silver medal was presented, and we clustered around our host, who was then near the peak of his public recognition. A leader in insouciance, I pressed the chairman to see if he would present us with one of his cigars, his familiar mass-media trademark. He was ready for the request (a predictable one from visiting yokels?) and handed out a couple. Just ordinary A & C panatelas, nothing like a really good Jamaican or Cuban-seed from the Dominican Republic. (It was comforting at the time, but later I noticed him on television smoking a large, black cigar that had never seen the inside of a cellophane wrapper, nor rested in the cigar rack at Drug Fair.) Gawking, presenting, and celebrity interviewing done, we retraced our path back to the basement, got in the van, and headed up to Capitol Hill for the next visit—this one with our congressman.

He had laid on lunch for us in a room off one side of a busy, gaudily painted corridor on the House side of the Capitol. The table and chairs alone nearly filled the room, and the food was predictable, but we were still excited and elated by our contact with what before had been remote and merely spoken of. The false familiarity implied by easy use of the nickname "the Fed" had been dispelled for us. "The Fed" was not just a phrase or an image, it was a place and it involved real people; we were witnesses to it in all its glory.

But surely this is surrendering to silliness. The reality of the Federal Reserve System (more correctly, its Board of Governors) is not gleaming marble, solicitous staff, and sunlit shrines. Rather, it is decisions and interest rates and all that—isn't it?

None of us seemed to feel that way. It was a place, and an impressive one. What if there is some connection, some unexplicated relation between where the governors meet, how they see themselves, and what they do? Is it possible that there is some tie between the governors and the superbaronial hall where they make their decisions, lordly and aloof from the crowd? Public decisions, not just those made by "the Fed," but all of the decisions made by governing bodies across the country about public finance—the long, benumbing, lists of figures—mean something in the lived world. They are how track is kept of people and materials and how their use is assigned. And all of this is done by people who seem to take cues from others and from their surroundings.

Another example, much closer to the actual work of city government: the architecture (well, interior decoration, at least) of municipal creditworthiness. The interview rooms at the two major bond-rating agencies in New York aren't grandiose. They're just quiet, stylish, and immaculately kept, but like the Federal Reserve headquarters, they radiate a sense of stability and settled authority. The actual business of rating bonds is straight-forward enough. The city has to borrow to pay for major construction projects. The cheapest way to borrow is to sell bonds, but the city's credit rating must be established before the bonds are sold. The better the rating, the less the amount of interest that must be paid to the borrowers and the less the annual debt payments. Part of the process of getting bond ratings involves face-to-face interviews with researchers in the New York head-quarters of the two major rating agencies, so four of us made the trek to the home of American money, Wall Street.

The weather was warm, May's promise and threat of Manhattan sum-mer heat to come. We stayed in a midtown hotel (new, but the elevators did manage to break down while we were there), took hot, noisy taxi rides, and endured similar routines at each place. The lobbies of the office buildings reflected their age—fifty or so years—in their spacious, polished-stone, plutocratic-baroque style; they were only a little marred by the bulky desks of the security guards. P., our bond adviser, knew the pro-cedure, cleared us through, and got us to the elevators and out on the proper floor. At one agency, the corridors were lined with false columns that were shiny and new, done in deep burgundy, as if to say, "Don't have shiny art-deco columns where you come from, huh?" At the other agency, the columns were a more discreet light gray, imparting an aura of tasteful simplicity.

The procedure at both places was to appear at the receptionist's desk, be identified, and then get ushered into an interview room furnished with a table just long enough to seat the group, leaving one or two extra chairs. At the first agency, there were black chair-rails on the light-gray wall, with wainscoting and a carpet done in darker gray. The chairs around the pol-ished, substantial table were moderately padded (be comfortable, but don't relax!) under a slightly rough, deep-burgundy fabric, all sleek and mod-ern—a credenza bore a shiny, chrome, insulated coffeepot and china cups and saucers; lights were behind shiny metal grills mounted flush with the ceiling; and a video monitor (did some clients bring taped presentations?) was recessed in the wall behind a screen. Everything was understated and discreet except the clock; large and round, it protruded from the wall. It had a plain face with large, fully represented black numerals and clearly visible hour, minute, and second hands—no need for a sign reminding anyone in this room that "Time Is Money." The only other representational decorations at the first agency were three pictures of three different sets of southwest-Indian baskets.

The pictures in the next agency were a collection of views of St. Stephen's Green, Dublin. There was a map, showing the park in an aerial view, rendered in pen and ink, with trees and paths stylized in the manner of an architect's sketch plan. A couple of pictures more, one (or was it both?) done in watercolors, with rich, luminous greens, reminiscent of an Irish summer. Could it be a lesson? Someone's creditworthiness may look lush and verdant from one perspective, white and skeletal from another? The walls of this agency's room were different too: ivory with no chair rail or wainscoting. The lighter, grayish burgundy of this set of (again) moderately padded swivel chairs was matched by the carpet. P. and I went to the rest room afterward (two overweight, middle-aged dogs leaving their scent marks); it was spotlessly clean and the decor was finished off with burnished brass fixtures at the wash basins.

They were just settings, but stylized to the point of ritual, turned into ceremonies that brought together more than the mere behaviors of the ceremony itself. But what is the *mysterium tremendum* (if any) that was not to be grasped directly but approached obliquely, through ceremony? The interviews were conducted with courtesy and precision. At the first agency there were two interviewers. One was blond, jovial, and beefy; the other was short, dark, and intense. We exchanged a few pleasantries, then they got down to the business of quizzing us. And so it went.

Lord knows the staff had sweat blood getting the information together for the official financial statement that had to accompany the request for a rating. Playing the role of elected official, I was along more to chime in at the appropriate times on matters of policy and politics. (The official statement listed the members of city council and their length of service: "As you can see, the city government is quite stable.") P., who had seen it all, served as a mother hen; W. had typically overprepared and cooked himself into a state of slightly jangled nerves. It was good for the presentation, but not so good for him—he looked tired and underexercised. H. was always a little harder to read—short, heavy, and talkative, he remained resolutely southern in the big city, discursive, pulling out spread sheets and reports, offering information until his questioner began to get that glazed-eye look that comes from eating too much. The official statement, the basis for the interviews, had more straight information on fewer pages than any other municipal document. Curiously, I'm the only one I know who used it to bone up when I had to give a speech on the city. The first interview proceeded, with W., H., and P. in dark business suits, good shirts, and silk ties. Just to give the air of being slightly unimpressed, I wore a tan suit.

How do we make an aging, industrial city with some transportation deficiencies look like a rosy investment prospect? Easy answer: Stress the positive. Part of the proposed loan was designated for airport improvements, so we made sure they knew about the increase in boardings and the sweeping extent of the improvements. That discussion led into politics, since one of the keys to this physical improvement was the rather complex agreement we had worked out with the county where the airport is located about the superficially unrelated matter of annexation. But who cares about the arcana of local intergovernmental relations? We tried to explain a little, especially about additional locally generated resources for the project by mentioning the travel promotion program, the visitors' center, and more. We responded to questions about the flood, the layoffs at Gem Manufacturing, the adequacy of the city's cash balances, the growth of receipts, and so on.

The interview at the second agency seemed to go well, too. One interviewer had attended college near the city, and so there was no need to explain to him the peculiarities of the area, its idiosyncratic politics, and its deeply rooted ease at feeling superior to anyplace else. P. had predicted a short interview, "just a half hour or so," but it ran the usual length—a little short of an hour and a half. Cash balances, internal financial reporting, the new accounting system, the flood again. And since the interviewer concluded with some guarded yet positive remarks, P. managed to look actually happy, a notable event.

But what of the place and what of the ritual? They were informational sessions to be sure, but they were not reducible to so many bits of information passing from one subject to another. What more is in the small, formal rooms, the elaborate courtesy and underlying insistence of the interviewers, and our nervous preparation? Why the careful construction of symbols in words, in movements, in decor? These are all the more effective because we talk as if they aren't there, and we pretend that economics and credit and finance are preeminently matters of individuals and wants, not sets of precariously constructed cultural artifacts like Anasazi baskets, products of a time and place that will never be duplicated. How odd that we are able to see all of this style and artifice as something that "naturally" developed out of the autochthonous working of "human nature." Perhaps these trips are like trips to conventions: you make the trip, carefully attend the appropriate speeches, sessions, and meals, and then agree with everyone else that the "real stuff" goes on elsewhere, in the conversations over drinks, in the contacts renewed and made, in the array of interchanges and speculations and news that doesn't have to be any of those things. It can be chitchat, time-killing, undirected bull sessions, or whatever the participants make of them.

We went back to the hotel for checkout and an upscale California cuisine lunch. Big white napkins were placed in our laps by the waitress, with the predictable wisecracks once she was out of earshot. The place even had little black licorice-flavored things like M & M's as part of their after-lunch breath-freshener selection. The taxi ride to the airport was hot and bumpy; our excitable driver almost managed to get in a fistfight and precipitate two collisions.

The airport terminal was showing its age. The rest room seemed in need of continuous maintenance, even though it was reasonably clean. (Thorstein Veblen update: the index of conspicuous consumption is no longer the expansive private residential lawn; in these days of institutional wealth, it's rest rooms that indicate how much surplus a given institution can devote to pure amenity.) There was one ingenious effort: someone had installed dark cork tiles over the urinals with front pages from various sections of the New York Times posted on them—sports, business, and general news. It evidently worked; there were no graffiti. But it was still a sign of penury. Lacking money, whoever did that was thrown back on using intelligence to maintain a degree of propriety.

W. and I had been talking as we walked down the corridors and passageways behind H. and P., debriefing ourselves and trying to refocus on what we were going back to. "Good story. I think we had a lot of good information. We really ought to get it circulated back home." He was right. The employment situation, even with the much-publicized and much-discussed layoffs, was better than most people realized. "An exercise like this makes you concentrate on what's really going on." One of the others said, "Yeah. You can't hand those guys a load of crap. Gotta know what you're talking about." "Uh-huh. And almost nobody back home even wants to pay attention. . . ."

W. had been worrying about public misperceptions, more properly nonperceptions, about how the city's finances and budget policies fit with economic activity in Hill City and the surrounding area. Without his putting it into words, I could guess what he was thinking. It seemed like we had worked, worried, studied, and worked some more to develop a carefully integrated, publicly acceptable set of policies governing the city's getting and spending of money. We had studied the impact of those policies on the community, refined planning techniques, made local politics and the economy work together, and come up with what seemed to us to truly be a remarkable blend of sophistication and hometown preferences. But the public's and the media's taste for discussing and criticizing all this seemed unable to rise any higher than an elemental concatenation of clichés and the universal political question, "What have you done for me lately?" There was no sense at all of what I guess we had hoped for but had never even dared to express: "Hey, look at what we (little ol' us!) can do with public finance!"

What W. did in fact do was remind me of something I had said at the recent council meeting where we had voted on the final adoption of the budget. Councilman J. had been delivering himself of some traditional utterances, voicing his doubt that the amount proposed was as little as possible—simple enough to say and a commonplace observation. I had made a short-tempered and fairly lengthy response, pointing out that the growth in spending was within the limits the council had set a full year before, that the council's major priorities had gotten enough resources, and that the point of a budget was to fund the responsibilities of government in keeping with the broad preferences of the community. Further, I argued that balancing all of this within limited resources was a considerable accomplishment, especially when you see how the clowns in Washington do it, or, for that matter, the state capital. And having gotten that "on the record," I had promptly dismissed it, but W. had thought about it.

One of the odd things about public statements is the way audiences interpret them—a good reason to be careful, almost guarded, and never to resort to "B.S.ing." Someone is listening, and taking what official X says very seriously, from a perspective X may know nothing about. It's best to speak only when you have something worth saying. W. was complimentary, but the real compliment lay in the fact that what I had said in the mild heat of a very short debate had started him thinking. "You know, people think that 'the budget' is the document—it's not." He had even worked out a metaphor: "The family snapshot is not the family!" He went on to explain himself. The budget, the "real" budget, not the snapshot encapsulation of it in a two-inch-thick document, is something much larger, far more complex, and quite different from the neat abstractions of line-items and dollar amounts. "The budget" is not one year's carefully bundled set of decisions; it is the stream of them, year after year, blending people, objects, and expectations. It is, tangibly and practically, how satisfied the people we hire are with their pay and their jobs, whether the garbage trucks with the perpetually squealing brakes get fixed, and how different people feel about the community. Each part affects the other—the employees' condition of employment affects how they treat the equipment; that influences what people think of city government and where they are, and so on.

But the document, the little stack of paper that we refer to as "the budget," exerts its talismanic power. Required by state law and a law itself after it is passed, seemingly a dry catalog of numbers punctuated by bureaucratic prose, it looks innocuous enough—heavy paper covers and a cheap plastic binding ring. Inside, there is black ink on white paper except for the yellow pages for income summaries and blue pages for expenditure summaries. Last year the cover was light blue; this year it's white with bright blue trim and the city's seal. The bulk of the pages present separate categories of expenditure, page after page: expenditure code 05205, "Emergency Communications," a total of $572,957 for the coming fiscal year— $427,373 for pay ("personnel services"), $10,070 for "supplies and materials," and so on. Only a small amount for the next entry, "Circuit Court," since the state pays most of that, though that's not noted in the meticulous document. Then the "General District Court" entry, and so on, all the way to the end—almost $4.5 million for debt service. Surely this document is a "bottom line" of some kind, a numerical essence that captures the whole?

But no—W.'s line again—"The snapshot is not the family!" It's odd to reflect that the snapshot, the Brownie camera with easily developed film and all of that, was invented at the same time as the executive budget, the now-typical way of preparing government budgets. Maybe that's the value of the budget as a document; with it a snapshot of city's finances is possible, and maybe that's more important than the precise details of its execution. (Hmmm; ground's tilted and it's a little overexposed, but you can tell it's her, even with her head cocked over to the side like that. . . .) It is more important to probe the implication of freezing, for one moment, things that in reality are unfreezable and unstoppable. Thus, the idea of suspending movement at one point, in effect, of stepping outside time to gain a perspective otherwise beyond reach—surely that is at the very least an adept administrative-legislative maneuver to reduce the real to the understandable and the manipulable.

To the extent that it achieves that end, "the budget" is an exercise in a certain kind of power. And possibly that is why it tends to be turned into an object of veneration apart from what it represents, ironically in danger of losing its potency as a tool to the extent that it is idolized, becoming just another statutory requirement or even a fetish. Maybe it is the numbers that scare most people in this age of growing mathematical illiteracy. A few, of course, are at home with the numbers to the point where they seem like esoteric knowledge, a set of secret keys to the universe. This is equally an error. And so the numbers in the document are taken for more than they are, and the confusion is compounded by thinking that it's a technical, numerical matter and hence a job for technicians that is of no public concern. And, of course, this misses the startling recognition that the budget document is not only law and figures: it is part of a ceremony, an act of communal representation. But if it's a ceremony, what are the commitments affirmed by it?

Over drinks in the airport lounge it didn't take much to get H. and P. to talk about their commitments to the budget, including keeping the figures straight, reaffirming that "you can't hand 'em a load of crap," and more. With some vigor they recounted stories of catching department heads trying, in effect, to switch funds from one account to another. P. recalled eavesdropping on a conversation over the city's two-way radio frequency by two employees trying to charge a purchase to an account other than the correct one because the incorrect account had more money in it. He had put a stop to it, and he summarized his wisdom on such matters: "If you're in a job to tell someone 'No,' goddamnit, ya gotta tell 'em 'No'!"

Technical skill with the numbers, the subject on which most public discussion comes to rest, is only the starting point to those who must use that skill on a daily basis in contact with the daily realities of the "real" budget, the lived one rather than the document. H. wanted to stress fiduciary responsibility—making sure not just that no one's stealing dollars but that what's spent is spent in accordance with the budget document's prescriptions. In his words, there is a commitment to "stewardship and responsibility for honesty and legal expenditure," a commitment that is a moral matter, not subject to the entreaties by fellow employees to do otherwise. P.'s formulation of the attitude necessary in the finance officer's position: "If you're a nice guy, you're gonna get the shit beat outta ya."

More conversations, more stories, such as the one about the nearby jurisdiction that had its water bills written out in pencil on sheets of paper—no billing system, no duplicates—and then had a water system employee who made out bills on his own, collected them, and pocketed the money for himself. There was technical talk about technical problems—the pressure of audits, last year's severe inventory embarrassment, the issue of comingling of funds, the puzzle of how to allocate costs for the use of a single facility among multiple users, the need for enough but not too many written records. Finally, it was time to catch the plane back, get off at our small, worn, familiar airport, tired and a little loopy—time to go home.

A final architectural note, this one from the auditorium in which we hold public hearings on the budget: from our seats on the stage, in the bright glare of the theatrical lights, the back of the auditorium seems to melt into a dim horizon, row after row of clean, well-kept seats progressively receding from view, finally becoming obscure in the shadows under the overhang of the balcony. Lots of seats, but very few people in them, very few. This had to have been the lightest turnout ever; only a handful of people in the 2,500 seats of the auditorium—a few spectators, a gaggle of school administrators, the standard quota of reporters. Only two people had come to speak at this, the annual public hearing on the combined city, school, and utility budget of over $65 million, and, as it turned out, these two hadn't come to the public hearing on the budget to talk about the budget at all. The members of the school board, who customarily sat with us at this annual meeting, had conducted a separate public hearing of their own on a different topic earlier in the day. That hearing had been on a proposed sex-education program, and time had run out before the two well-dressed black women had had their chance to speak. They particularly wanted to respond to some white fundamentalists who had evidently monopolized the discussion. Consequently, here they were, getting their arguments in at this hearing. B., presiding, said nothing, and we heard them quietly. In the great cavernous auditorium, with radio, television, and newspaper reporters ready to publicize any comment anyone might care to make, to give it weight and prominence just because it would have been something to report, no one had anything to say.

It was quite a contrast to what had been the case just a few years back. One of the last budget hearings we had in a smaller room had been in the middle-school cafetorium. The room had been packed, and it was hot, crowded, and noisy. B., the spokesman for the local taxpayers' movement, in one of his last public displays, paced the aisles with a large, stuffed toy monkey on his back, shouting: "Get the monkey off my back! I've got to get the tax monkey off my back!" The crowd reacted, adding both cheers and derisive comments, stimulating him to carry on, while the toy monkey watched it all with a fixed, manic grin, bouncing around on B.'s heaving back as he moved around the room. B.'s group had gotten started several years earlier, when real estate values had risen suddenly with real estate taxes following suit. The bulk of his supporters had been, like him, retired homeowners, and those I knew personally seemed to live frugally, though he had some wealthy patrons who evidently shared his populist disdain for "the country-club set." He had some moments of prominence in connection with some earlier controversies, but real estate taxes had stabilized, and generous tax relief for the elderly had been enacted, taking the sense of urgency from his appeal. That night, the furor had been directed at nothing, and the proposed budget had passed with little change. For this hearing, there was no crowd at all. One city hall perspective: "If a hundred people show up for a hearing, that's a big crowd in a small room. If a hundred people show up in a big auditorium, you begin to realize that in a city of seventy-five thousand people, a hundred isn't very many. Public hearings are fine, but we're as responsible to those who don't show up at hearings as to those who do."

Noted as part of a conversation about how Valley City moved this year's budget hearing to a nine-thousand-seat civic arena: a crowd of pay-hungry teachers and a large number of restaurant owners and employees protesting meal taxes came, and on the television screen all looked lost in the immensity of the hall. The council passed its budget as presented. But what does this kind of manipulation add up to? Genuine insight and a defensible way to keep from merely having to grease the wheels that are currently squeaking the most? Or less, just a rationalization of a clever grasp of the psychology of crowds and space . . . or something else? A decade ago, the annual adoption of our budget was typically a strained, turbulent affair. Now, peace and quiet. Seemingly, such a change would be the topic of at least some local conversation—street talk—but it's not, as near as I can tell. At least A. likes to talk about the change and keep track of how it continues to evolve, so we occasionally mull it over.

The change had begun a decade ago with a head-on collision between the city manager and the "new" city council over the kind of financial information the administration would provide the council and how the budget would be adopted. Because the city manager was both decent and competent, and because the council had a clear sense of what it wanted to do, the fight made sense and had an outcome. Councilman O., with two master's degrees and a military background, used the sophisticated computer system at the research and design facility where he worked to challenge some of the estimates provided by the administration and to set a high standard for the future generation of information. (Of course, O. is gone now, and the computer facility has been relocated to Texas. None of what happened could have happened if they had not been here at just that time: a conjunction of personal, corporate, and civic orbits at that political instant made it possible.) Among other things, I had insisted on advance, legislated growth limits, the political key to making the technical changes workable over time. The limits were simple enough—at the same time the budget was passed for the upcoming year, we enacted a growth limit for the year after that. That way, everyone who looked to the budget would be warned that there wouldn't be a cornucopia for them the next time, but if someone didn't spend all their appropriation, they could use it for innovations that the modest annual increases would not otherwise allow. Everyone ended up with a vested interest in keeping track of projections and planning. The public got assurances that the overall fisc was under control. But S. had been beside himself, outvoted at the meeting when we first adopted two-year limits, but he was ready enough later to take credit for the way they led to the elimination of gamesmanship and short-term politicking.

For example, the school board had been in the habit of regularly requesting $300,000 for a planetarium, and so the council just as regularly cut it from the request with a certain amount of fanfare about cutting things by a third of a million dollars—without actually cutting anything. No more of that, and a similar discipline was applied to train (too strong a word?) department heads to ask for what their operation required, not to pad their requests in anticipation of being cut so that they would get what they thought they could reasonably expect to begin with. (W. again, always thoughtful, watching: "Trust! The essence of budgeting that makes sense is trust, and the problem is how to build it!")

Somehow the refinements, over time, put an end to legislative posturing and nickel-and-diming, and they put the focus on overall control. A bad example from years back at a hearing and work session on a proposed budget: Councilman D., manager of the large, profitable Acme store, a genuine civic leader—decent, concerned, and not given to futile gestures—led the review of the proposed budget by concentrating on the details, making the common (and wrong) assumption that "if you take care of the pennies, the dollars will take care of themselves." The police department had requested nearly a hundred dollars apiece for protective screens to install between the front and back seats of the squad cars to protect the drivers from unruly prisoners, but D. had decided that that was a lot of money for a screen. The police chief responded, "Yessir, we thought so too, but they're about the only supplier in the country, and it would cost a lot more to make 'em ourselves." Silence. End of discussion. D. had, no doubt, poured over the document for hours and had come up with a suspected savings of . . . how much? Maybe fifty bucks a screen, times twenty squad cars for a hoped-for total savings of a thousand dollars? Out of a budget that was running back then at maybe $25 million or more? D. had just been deflated—he didn't get even that paltry thousand dollars. He must have felt frustrated, to have put so much into an effort to exercise his authority publicly, to try to be seen as responsible and disciplined, and to have it fall so flat. Did he sense that under the details some unmanageable problems were accumulating? We later figured out that the city's expenditures had been growing much faster than dependable revenues. Put in human terms, people were regularly expecting more from city hall than they were willing to pay for. That, in conjunction with other matters, later led to the untimely ends of some political careers.

Yet on that night no one had complained. There were no complaints about wasted time and effort; no complaints about lack of results; no distress that the men elected to govern ("hardheaded practical business-men") were doing little more than executing a series of painful, hollow gestures while the problems with which they alone could have come to grips simply accumulated. What could have been going through their minds as—or if—they reflected on what they were doing? Did any of them sense that by taking on the role of junior auditors they had effectively abdicated their authority over much more?

Ritual, place, meaning: it's not at all odd to consider the context if we want to consider the doing of a budget and not just engage in a display of economic or quantitative rhetoric. Most people seem to prefer the rhetoric in fairly pure form, not mixed with considerations of resources, commitments, and so forth. Better the sound and the fury than a potentially entangling contact with what the sound and the fury are supposed to signify.

It goes without saying that there is no written history of how what should have been a passing local political crisis became the beginning of a series of changes and refinements that would be, eventually, simply the way things were done. It was a series of arrangements and deliberate plans that fit together, discouraged game-playing and nit-picking, and let major decisions be treated as major decisions. As a result, decisions on infrastructure projects, agreements on construction schedules, what the council said, what it directed the administration to focus attention on, and how it rated the manager became the major priorities for the year. All the changes followed from one to another, gave a sense of the timing of what would happen to the public, and avoided commitments that couldn't be carried out. ("Trust! The essence of budgeting that makes sense is trust!") My own role became little more than reminding people of their roles, "taking the point" against proposals to fund projects outside the policies that the council had agreed upon, and occasionally puzzling over what needed to be adjusted to keep it all running. And I infrequently ponder how the original, incredibly prosaic goal of balancing income and outgo became obscured, replaced in sense of importance with how the sets of commitments and plans became the tools for identifying new projects and fresh variations in the community's sense of self, as well as keeping as best we could the massive commitments already made.

If finance is partly a matter of keeping track of the dollars—uniform, equal, absolutely quantifiable dollars—then it is also a matter of something that cannot be reduced to the verities of manuals and textbooks and published standards. The experience of actually working with these things, in a lived context, demonstrates that it is also a matter of people and their commitments, how they see themselves and what they do, and the value of all these. If public finance is partly a matter of legislated budgets and accounting systems and audits—fixed, identifiable, down-in-black-and-white legal documents—then it is also a matter of how those things are used by the people who have to work within the institutional boundaries, how the public understands what is and is not there, and how politics works. No set of categories, no matter how carefully gleaned from the documents, can purport to convey useful information about budgets unless it acknowledges the pervasive influence of the felt environment—not just people and wants, but the attitudes, the common sense of possibilities and prohibitions, and a strong sense of the future, or at least "what it'll be like next year." Even the physical setting has importance in these non-numerical but very concrete ways.

Said to A., after he had made reference to "our budget system," with a pause afterward, as if he thought he had said something wrong: "Y'know, we've got a system that's not a system." And with a sudden smile of satisfaction he replied, "Yeah."

A lot of people seem to think that the height of intelligence is to become a specialist, an expert who can master something more thoroughly than anyone else can master it. Why? To be able to make that most compelling of claims, the claim to know something so completely that the expert's word must be taken as truth, with no debate and no challenge: I know, you obey. That is an enticing vision to carry around in one's head, watching everyone fall down in awe of sheer, unarguable truth. If knowledge is power, then it would be sovereign power, if only over a tiny realm. Sadly for the vision, what we are called on to do is not much like that. If expertise is necessary—and it is—and if those who are called on to make governmental judgments have to have both their own expertise and broad knowledge on top of it, expertise turns out to be the starting point, not the end. In the end, we are always brought back to the context of Hill City itself—where the different perspectives and foci fit together. Not just finance, but engineering, sociology, law, medicine, and art, too, not to mention the capacity to assess other people, and maybe even being lucky or gifted with insight. The expertise of government and politics makes sense only if it allows the others to fit together, to make their own contributions. To be useful, specialized knowledge has to remain aware of its own limits, to recognize the embracing context. It is its context that establishes the meaning of an activity and that is its chief defense against becoming a self-absorbed absurdity.

FIVE

Auctoritas

An intelligent person remains sane by rejecting the childish collages
of strength and compassion which the authorities present as pictures
of themselves. Yet our rejection is not connected with seeing
a better image of authority in the mind's eye. And our
need for authority as such remains.

—Richard Sennett, *Authority*

The guidebook stated that it was one of the largest forts along Hadrian's
Wall. Since it was a half-mile off the road, we had to park the car and walk
to it through erratic gusts of cold rain. In my perverse taste in weather, I
relished it; if M. minded much, she was too game to let on. The rain was a
fit introduction to a lifeless high-water mark of a vanished empire, and I
could hear in my mind a counter-tenor chorus chanting the old ninth-
grade jeer:

> Latin is a dead language
> Dead as it can be!
> It killed off all the Romans
> And now it's killing me!

Maybe the shade of Miss Miller, my long-deceased Latin teacher, would
approve of this little hike more than she approved of my classwork. We
walked quickly, around knots of nervous, disdainful sheep, and climbed
over a knoll, out of sight of cars, highway, and parking lot. In predictable
British fashion, the ruins were painstakingly preserved. The exposed foundations of the old garrison buildings and the remaining parts of their walls
had been firmly cemented to forestall further decay. Neat signs marked the
points of interest around the fort. The omnipresent grass covered the soil
in a smooth, even carpet—green grass, white stones, gray sky. The puddles
of rainwater gleamed with a metallic luster, and the long wall itself, deli-
cately fringed with the black sticks and twigs of the still-leafless trees,

seemed to march down the swale and up the next hill, off on some mission of its own that had outlived the purposes of the engineers who had planned and directed its construction.

Think of those long-dead engineers, far from home, beset by a gloomy, wet climate and tribes of uncouth natives. Whoever they were, they had taken part in activities that added up to organizing and governing. Without dynamite or diesel engines (but with . . . what? whips and swords? impressed labor, slaves taken in war, bored legionnaires?) they quarried the stone and did the construction. Without newspapers, radio, or TV, they kept a sure grasp on the course of events and shaped the world to the image of their mother Rome, the original City of Seven Hills. How could they keep their presence of mind and at the same time make such exertions so far from the warm, sunny Mediterranean? How could they and their ancestors have turned several square miles of unimpressive Italian countryside into the heart of a world empire? The present-day keepers of the ruins had even excavated the square stone sewer that served the fort, reminding us that whatever sense of exaltation and duty drove those vanished, unfathomable Romans, they were still able to accommodate the mundane in a tidy, urbane way.

But the mute landscape answered no questions; it remained only a somberly composed reflection of mortality—*sic transit gloria mundi*. So we hurried back down the hill to the car as the rain and wind picked up. According to the guidebook, there was a museum down the way that might offer some more clues; an anaerobic bog had preserved for nearly two thousand years some perishable items from a nearby garrison settlement—scraps of Roman leather and textiles, a centurion's storehouse inventory, a gracefully made lady's sandal—relics of the means and ends that so possessed those ancient conquerors and builders, now so lost to our awareness. (They will soon be finally lost to any wonder or reflection at all, never again to live in any new generation's imagination as "the great ones who went before.") A centurion's storehouse inventory—prosaic and dull, a humdrum reminder that successful warfare was more than the test of battle, more than the shouting and hacking with short, well-sharpened swords in the ditch in front of the camp, relentlessly beating back the passionate onslaught of the tribes. After battle and burials there would be armor to repair, swords to replace or resharpen, food to allocate—the ordinary, undramatic necessities that would secure what had been won and make the next battle possible. And someone had to keep track of it all to make sure that the scarce supplies were not wasted but served the task at hand, that pilferage and thievery were kept in check.

The lady's sandal—not a boot or a slipper but an open sandal—was not a work shoe but almost an ornament, surely worn for no heavier task than shopping in the little market behind the protection of the wall and the legions. Perhaps it had merely allowed its wearer to be seen as delicate and civilized. Would a woman have brought it and its vanished mate all the way from Rome, traveling north with the army? Or would one of the more docile local girls have been ready to become a centurion's mistress and adopt Italian styles? It was an artifact of a peaceful life, maybe even an indulgent life—Venus with a shopping basket on her arm, a complement to Mars in the storehouse taking inventory.

When the legions left, after several centuries, it was on summons from the metropolis, not from rebellion by those they had conquered long before. Their departure was mourned, and, not long after, an era of banditry and struggle fell over the countryside of villas and farms and the Romano-Britannic towns and cities that had grown from the military camps. The garrisons were deserted, and no doubt the unpatrolled walls soon started to fall into disrepair. A muddy, booted, warlike time was at hand. Whatever the Roman power was—unparalleled military tenacity, stern-yet-equitable law, clear and logical language, eminently practical and productive engineers and builders, times so peaceful that domestic life could be preoccupied with itself—it vanished. Only a scattering of the power's traces were left behind, not the power itself.

We got to the museum too late to get in, so we drove to the next town and found a handsome little inn where we ate indulgently and slept well into the morning. Leaving reveries of antiquity behind, we drove south toward York and the Middle Ages.

Another image of power, this one American and from the early part of our own century: the familiar photo of President Theodore Roosevelt seated at the controls of a steam shovel at a Panama Canal construction site. The image is more than photochemically induced shadows on film or a glass plate; it is a grand summation and a signpost. It shows the hero of San Juan Hill, the harbinger of Progress, leading the conquest of what had cost the fortunes, hopes, and lives of all who had tried it before. Three centuries after Drake, the photo reveals another English-speaking raider working his will on this undeveloped Hispanic country: Theodore Roosevelt, of the teddy bear and the first presidential news conference, in a rumpled white suit, seated stiffly at the control levers of a steam shovel symbolizing the greatest construction project in the world.

The photograph is not technically good; it is grainy and imprecise. Yet

for those willing to consider it, it crystallizes a host of purposes and
metaphors, surely not lost on Roosevelt, the photographer, or the adoring
public. He was the popular leader of a mass democracy in charge of an
unprecedented and monumental engineering project that would serve our
convenience, security, and prosperity. It is an image of the Age of Power.
"Congress debated; I acted." (When did we start to call electricity "the
power," to identify the exercise of our will not with physical compulsion
or moral suasion but with the management of technology?)

Roosevelt was the trustbuster as well, summoning the power of the
people to combat the power of the great new industrial and financial
corporations. Does the picture show us something we didn't expect? Was
there more of a connection than anyone had recognized between harness-
ing technology to create a power that could transform our material existence and that other effort, the creation of a new political power for the
transformation of our civic existence? Roosevelt, sitting at the control
levers of that new replacement for men and muscle, the steam shovel—
capable of moving dirt by the cubic yard, not just by the shovelful. Aimed
at home consumption, the image also must have resonated in political life,
a reminder of mass communication, of public opinion, of a new political
power to be created for the new century. For our more obscure and local
concerns it is enough to remember that Roosevelt was also a member of
the National Municipal League, one of the most successful organizations
among those that sought to change city politics. And our city's politics
were changed by men who were knowledgeable enough to both admire
and resent Theodore Roosevelt, I think.

That old photograph remains just that, an old image from another
time. But in the file in front of me lay a more tangible collection of evidence, correspondence from a long-dead librarian of our privately endowed
library, carefully typed, outlining his conscientious tracking of the nation-
wide civic reform movement. There were reports on the National Municipal League conventions of 1907 and 1908 and a bibliography compiled by
the chief bibliographer of the Library of Congress, with articles from such
journals as *McClure's* and *American Political Science Review.* Also included
was a list of books about reform available then in our library, including
Deming's *Government of American Cities,* Goodnow's *City Government in the
United States,* and Bradford's *Our Failures in Municipal Government.* Roosevelt's Progressives, here in our dusty local archives! The librarian had not
been acquiring these for the sake of acquisition, though. A copy of his
letter to a local business leader, chairman of the Committee on Govern-

ment by Commission, was in the file, too, carefully directing the chairman to the library resources that were available to assist him in the struggle to create a new form of government for Hill City.

R., in his oddly diffident way, must have done some extra work to unearth this, showing it to me in the musty reading room of the decrepit library building, a room that smelled of old books and yellowing paper. It was mostly quiet and generally the haunt of genealogists and tourists prowling through lists of veterans of various wars and colonial tithables or ransacking local histories for mentions of their ancestors.

The movement to get a commission form of government, patterned on that of Galveston, Texas, must have died out, fallen apart, or been absorbed by a successor group. It would be over a decade from the time the librarian started meticulously compiling information and corresponding with interested citizens until a reform government was actually adopted. It should have been possible to find out more, just by starting with the names of those citizens—their family names were the corporate names of this store, that shoe factory, and so on. But our local historians are not much interested in such complexities. Neither who did what nor how the local legislative, judicial, and executive institutions were profoundly reshaped are as attractive as personal drama, human interest, and local trivia. So, there is only the dim apprehension among the few remaining local owners of major local enterprises that the men they once looked to as fellow magnates—directors who worked great changes two generations ago—are dying off and not being replaced. Instead, their companies are being bought by corporations from outside, and their headquarters are being moved elsewhere.

From a private meeting, held in the boardroom of the bank building, of a business-based group that was struggling to find a way to exert itself in civic life: "You don't understand! You're not going to be able to raise the money; there's no one to go to anymore!" The speaker was one of the last of the old-style local owner-managers, racked by cancer himself, unable to imagine any other way of doing things for the city than the way he had done them for many years and with real generosity. Since precisely this problem—the lack of anyone "to go to"—lay at the core of what the group had been assembled for, no one said anything. The painfully slow, exploratory conversation moved on, and the speaker got up and left.

Evidently, that group of reformers from decades ago relied less on fanfare and more on the persistence of the local businessmen, absolute leaders of the city's manufacturing enterprises. It was a group that must have done a lot. The reform government that finally did get adopted was the council-manager form, invented up in the valley at about the same time the librarian was gathering information about the "Galveston experiment" to see if we should try it.

One of the accumulated pieces of information that must have been part of the process appeared in the local newspaper about halfway through this period: a speech given in another city by a civil engineer (an engineer— power over nature!) who had done work in town and had become a city manager in another state. He must have kept up his local contacts, for our newspaper reprinted most of his speech on his own city's experience with the council-manager form of government. Among other things, he noted:

> The work of all departments of city government [in his reformed city] was concentrated and made more compact than was possible under the former system of government. The heads of the various departments are hired by the city manager, and with him form a sort of a cabinet with which he keeps in close touch. To increase the friendly relations between city manager and the department heads, the city manager has entertained the heads at least once a month at a semi-official business and social gathering.

Likewise, Hill City acquired a coherent, consciously managed unit of government with a single executive leader, hired by a small council of elected lawmakers.

Seventy years later, the city manager, talking to me in his office in City Hall: "At the Monday morning staff meeting I try to get everyone thinking about their different problems. L. was worried about showing the site team raw land in the area designated to be the new industrial park—'You can't just point at a patch of woods and say it's all gonna be here. They have to at least be able to get into it.' B. jumped right in and said he could get some equipment right away and at least clear a jeep trail. . . ." He was rightly proud and a little excited about guiding the staff meetings so that they could be used both to discover and to remedy problems at the same time. Had this been merely fortunate, or his own idea? Was it something about getting people to work together he had picked up at one of the seminars he kept such careful track of? No matter. He paused for a moment, then summarized: "I don't think any organization in town but city government could have done that. . . . Realtors don't have bulldozers. . . . City government has a lot of different resources that you can use. . . ." And, he implied, if proper direction is given, those resources can be focused on the major tasks at hand. He was telling me this, I think, in part because he'd try things out on me every once in a while, but also because for four years running, the council as a whole had set economic development at the top of its annual priority list. He could well have been making the tacit report that he was getting department heads to work together on it, not just leaving it all to L. and his office.

That was how he was handling, in subtle and complex ways, the city manager's legal authority that is spelled out in such a different style in the city charter, in terse and complete legal language: "The City manager shall appoint all such city officials and employees as the council determines are necessary for the proper administration of the affairs of the city. . . . He shall have the power to discipline and remove every officer or employee so appointed by him."

Where are the images of power in this dry nest of words, that power that is so entrancing to the public eye? There is no publicity, no plaudits or criticisms, no great debates, no sweeping explications of the rise or fall of empires, no sense of global significance. Yet surely this all has something to do with power, though it is clearly not public power, pure and simple. In the above case—OK'ing the offer by the director of public works to help the economic development office by ordering in a bulldozer—power was just the ability to do something that needed doing right away. Doing it was simple if you had the resources to make it simple. But making it simple involved being part of an organization that was both large enough to have things like bulldozers and small enough to allow department heads to talk once a week or so about what was bugging them; all of this with a city manager who could hire and fire and a governing body that had clearly and repeatedly said that the community as a whole—not to mention the government—needed to pay a lot more attention to its economic future if it was going to have one.

Images of librarians, groups of local businessmen, and the daily conduct of administration sit uncomfortably beside visions of irresistible imperial legions or massive engineering projects that pierce continents in order to join oceans. But the change of the charter, now so completely taken for granted, and the expectation that a real manager would shape things up, was at one time new and noted in some detail. For example, in an early statement to the council, the first city manager reported that his management of the police force had "tightened up on such lax customs as wearing blouses unbuttoned, smoking on duty, and social visits." Apparently, the council and the attentive part of the public had expected such things back in 1920. They were not major items, even then, but they were still indica-

tive of the way things would be. Is the concern with such things too trivial
to be called "power"? Maybe it is just influence, or even more vaguely, just
a general change in the civic atmosphere? Had there been an election that
was the turning point or did it happen otherwise? Who had taken what
role? There must have been excitement, tension, a sense that a struggle
was going on and its outcome was in doubt, but I can't find many clues to
whatever the struggle was.

When the bunch of us got elected to the city council together, with
only one incumbent reelected, it had been exciting enough. On election
night we gathered at the suburban meeting hall of a civic club—a modest,
one-story cement block building, painted pale green and built strictly for
utility. The coalition leadership had been there from the time the polls had
closed one hour before, organizing what hopefully would be a victory
party and getting set to record and post the election returns for the waiting
crowd. Driving in too fast, I had to hit the brakes hard, sliding the car
through the gravel, bumping the old telephone pole that had been laid on
the ground to mark the edge of the lot. Tightening my tie, I jumped out
of the car and trotted in. The room was one-quarter filled: tense, and still
quiet. B. was there, so I went over to him. He had organized most of this,
skillfully and knowledgeably. He reassured me: "You don't have anything
to worry about. You're the one sure winner on the slate."

It was gratifying to hear, but nothing would soothe my inner turmoil.
All I could do was just wait and wait, agonizing because at that point there
was nothing else to do. Before election day, the campaign activities themselves offer opportunities to do something to counter candidate paranoia—
that cold, inner suspicion that nothing's working, that you'll lose. You can
shake more hands, pass out more cards, dream up more press releases, get
crazy ideas from the staff and volunteers, but on election day, there's no
point in doing anything. The ballots have all been cast. If you'd done what
you needed to do, it would turn out right. If it didn't turn out right, then
you'd know you hadn't done what you needed to do—too late to make
any difference. How many volunteers had actually handed out their literature? How many cards were still resting in stacks that hadn't been broken
since they left the printer?

In this election, what had the opposition really done? D., long regarded as the "power behind the throne," had started a whisper campaign—"radical, unreliable,"—probably more and probably to no effect,
but you never know. Why did I expose myself to all this, especially a
second time? Also, D. had been disdainful of those who did run, and he

had explained why his sons, by definition among those who "ought" to run, did not: "They shouldn't have to put up with all that crap. . . ." Public hearings and criticism, electoral campaigning—"all that crap." It seemed arrogant at the time, but indeed, why put up with it? Great confidence? Great need? The psyches of most candidates are probably ugly, but why dwell on it; everyone else's insides bleed and stink too, don't they? Whatever it looks like from the outside, campaigning is not just gregarious, extensive contact with others. It also probes a candidate's inner recesses, dredging out the tag ends of old fears and anxieties that finally get mixed up with some overwhelming desire for office, power, prominence, or simple recognition. Maybe it is just curiosity, or an impulse like Plato's simple, archaic refusal to be governed by those you know are worse than you are. It is too easy to reduce it to obvious material incentives, too easy to assume with ignorance and cynicism that it all reduces to calculable financial gain or personal power, and too obviously wrong when one notices how many officeholders settle for neither, but instead settle for tin-horn celebrity or some tawdry personal favors.

Whatever the case, forget it. Campaigning is work to do: "Good afternoon. I'm _____, and I'm running for city council. (Hand card to voter.) I sure would appreciate your vote on election day."

That's right—you have to ask for each vote. It's his or hers; it's part of each voting citizen. As a personal possession of someone else, it should be treated with respect. They shouldn't be expected to give them up without at least being asked; it's their consent, their little tokens of freedom in a world already too full of restraints. But an inner voice says: "Surely I don't need to do this grubby asking. If these people were really smart they would just flock in and vote for me because I'm so deserving." But another voice counters: "Yeah, sure. George Washington had to do it, and I have to do it. But unlike the Father of our Country, I haven't had to knock open a barrel of whiskey on the courthouse green. God and the Founding Fathers set it up the way that confronts me now, and though I'm not overly fond of it, I should try to see my way clear to approach those whose favor I am asking as if they are (or might be, or might want to be) free citizens, and as if I am too. But I should recognize that I will be bound to them as they are to me by the emblematic ceremony of voting. To hell with D. and his formulation, 'all that crap.'"

The returns started coming in. B., blind from a stroke, sat with the phone in the back room, carefully matching returns to projections. So far so good. O. was running a little ahead of where B. thought he would in

Hillside—good news. There were more returns, more favorable results. Well-wishers don't flock to the headquarters of losing candidates, but they do come to hang out around the winners. The crowd grew steadily and became more enthusiastic. There were reporters from newspaper, radio, and TV—cheers and waves as the TV camera got set up. My win was assured early. Fine. Still, waiting for the rest of the results was draining—for me, how the rest of the slate did could mean the difference between being taken seriously and being barely tolerated.

T. was in trouble. H. was barely ahead of V.—my God, if we couldn't beat V. after all that had gone on, capped with his public displays of pique. . . . O. was in great shape; J. was wiping out G. The crowd continued to build—hugging and cheering. A tiny, white-haired woman seized my arm, her eyes full of tears: "When I was fourteen I worked at the mill and had to leave town because I tried to organize a union. Now this is really my home again. . . ." She broke off with a sob, leaving me moved and puzzled. None of us were remotely pro-union; we were maybe a little populist in style, but nothing more. Unions weren't even a campaign issue, but she had gotten attached to us, fervently. The jubilation swelled: "Hooray, we got 'em!" "Good work, ol' buddy!"

But T. had clearly lost. He wandered around the room, disconsolate. He had greatly enjoyed campaigning and all the attention it brought. H. continued to hang on by a thread; he had to win if we were to have a majority. Finally, the last voting place called in. H. had beaten V.—by sixty votes. We had won. We had won big.

Amid all the campaign talk of how we could change things, it had been easy to focus on the petty personal defects of some of the incumbents, such as reading newspapers during meetings, dozing off, and arguing with citizens who spoke at council meetings. But we would have to work out what kind of change we would make and how it would happen. And that took considerable effort, as we found out later—much more than we knew then.

The election results in, we whooped and hollered our way out to the parking lot, gleefully piled into a single car, and headed for the television station and the election-night interviews. "Drive carefully now—you haven't been drinking, have you?" "Hell, we shouldn't all be in the same car; we're too valuable!" "A car must have two engines and a copilot—company policy. Hoo-eee!" Except for us, the streets were dark and quiet, black ribbons splashed by the blue-white circles under the streetlights. We got to the station in time to beat the deadline for the eleven o'clock news. Suppressing our own exuberance, we submitted to relatively sober interviews.

The oddest part of it all was the next day. Invitations to events I had never been invited to before began to arrive in a steady stream. Those who had been determined opponents the day before called with hearty congratulations, while a couple of what I had thought were my most enthusiastic supporters suddenly became calculating and guarded. Had I done or said something? Or was I finding out more about all of them, traits that it would be best to find out early? I found out who my most thoughtful and sympathetic friends were; they were the ones who passed my win off with either simple congratulations or a joke. But P. stopped me on the sidewalk to repeat Charles II's grim advice: "Keep your own counsel, and trust no one." As it turned out, those words were particularly applicable in his case.

W. called, a genuine old-timer, close to politics and scornful of the efforts of the "younger group." As one of the incumbents, he had lost, but not by much. Despite being sickly and possessed of a secretive political style, he had kept much of his following. But here he was, phoning congratulations and offering his advice whenever I wanted it. Startled, I thanked him too hastily and hung up. But the call from D. was even more surprising, and his chummy tone struck me as even more hypocritical than his message: "I just wanted to congratulate you and tell you I'm all for you. I had to be against you in the campaign, but I'm all for you now."

What kind of fool did he take me for? One of the wealthiest men in town, a long-time politico, generally regarded as powerful, he had for once been out-maneuvered, out-gunned, beaten. As near as I could tell, he had openly lied about answers I had given him to his "private" questions early in the campaign. Despite winning, it took the new council over a year to dig out from under the suspicion he had generated. All this, and here he was, telling me he "had" to be against me, though no one in town could force him to do anything. I said something pretty close to "Gee, thanks" and hung up.

No one in office (at least not anyone with any sense) talks much about "power." This custom particularly requires that the official talk about neither the power he thinks he has nor the power other people think he has. It's an act of arrogance to go so far as to murmur something like, "You've come to the right place," even when the occasion seems to call for it. But is that just more hypocrisy, the sort of disingenuousness that I found so distasteful in D.? A reflective person might well take this dissimulation as something much more than appropriate modesty, as a deceptively bland, public mask to guard a potentially sinister secret of the craft. That's not quite the case. Street talk portrays power, "clout," as a tangible thing that can be possessed by a person, as in "So-and-so has a lot of power," or, "How much clout does what's-his-name really have?," or, "Well, I know who has power in this community."

In all of these expressions, "power" is something that someone "has." Several years back, shortly after a chain bought out the local newspaper, the new owners devoted the better part of an entire issue to a description of our local "power structure." Rumor had it that this was standard practice for that chain—a surefire seller of papers and a way to become ingratiated both with those who get listed as being among the powerful and with that part of the general public that is always eager for gossip. Part of the buildup for the edition was a detailed description of how the study would be conducted—a panel would be assembled to screen nominees, then a wider panel would be polled to determine who "had power." "Power" was identified in exactly the way one might assess wealth—what person possessed "how much" of it. As the reporter who had responsibility for this respectfully noted, a well-known professor at Adjacent State University had devised this methodology. What the reporter failed to note (did he even know?) was that the procedure had been developed a generation ago and had been since subjected to extensive academic criticism. But that didn't matter. The study was popular, and it did fit exactly street talk's penchant for assuming that "power" is concrete and tangible, that it is owned and can be measured in terms of that ownership. (But what about street talk's other "power"—electricity, which we call "the" power. What if political power is more like electrical power—can a copper cable "have" electricity?)

Consider the example of S., who was in office when he made the "top ten" in the poll. I think it turned his head at the time. He was energetic, to the point of being frantic in the view of some, and had successfully promoted a couple of major projects and received appropriate public credit for doing so. Beaten in a race for higher office, he retired. Here's the strange part: he has scarcely been heard from since. If he "had power" in the sense of owning it, how could it vanish so quickly? Surprising, unless his power was not a personal possession but something that had to do with being in office, with how he used the office, with what all that was used for, with the character of the office itself and the capacities of the institution of which it was a part—the city government. Yet street talk still seems to want to talk about "power" in that tangible, possessory way: "Power?

Hell, he doesn't have any. Why go to him?" Power does have a decisive ring to it, used that way. It sounds definitive, real. That view of power even has some truth in it—just enough to breed illusions.

The collection of people who decided to oppose the market project in the name of historic preservation must have been thinking in some such terms. I don't know and won't ever find out, but the way they did what they did seemed to reflect a belief that there was a thing somewhere that a reasonable person could call power and could possess if he undertook the correct actions in the correct sequence. (Pause a moment, and smile. In politics, which is a fluid, protean activity with few fixed boundaries or prescriptions, there are people who are looking for a clear, one-two-three, step-by-step process with guaranteed results. They act like there's a handbook to follow.) At issue was a short row of vacant commercial buildings at a still-busy but declining downtown intersection. The buildings ranged in age from seventy to over a hundred and fifty years, and were empty, neglected, and forlorn.

Late in the affair, on a solo inspection tour, I stood on the darkened second floor of one of the buildings—windows bricked up, no electricity, no flashlight—noting that the only light I could see was coming from between the bricks. But it was the feel of the place that alarmed me. "Fine old building—just needs a little repair." Not likely: the engineers said it was on the verge of collapse, and I swear I could sense it through my skin. Nothing seemed solid—the firemen had already put us on notice that if the building caught fire, they would not go inside to try to save it. The steps I had to climb and the floor I was on vibrated in some range beyond hearing, seeming to announce the building was on the point of just letting go. Later, outside, I was able to match that unexpected cutaneous sense with a visual image: the wrecker's clamshell hitting the rear wall for only the second time, bricks from the wall arcing outward in a puff of dust, red bricks against a bright blue sky, no white mortar anywhere on them—a shower of single red bricks falling separately into a heap below. The ancient mortar had turned to sand; the wall had been held up by little more that its own weight and a tenuous skeleton of a few old, heavy beams.

The preservationists had good publicity early on. It's pretty easy to argue that something new need not be done, that the old can just be fixed up: "Cheaper that way, anyhow." The evolution of city hall's efforts to "do something" about that section of Main Street finally led to the decision to tear the buildings down so that room could be made for the renovation and expansion of the farmers' market. The architect hired for the job did very attractive renovation work, and he paid a lot of attention to the appearance of the new market—landscaping, a new fountain, attractive brick walls and walkways. It took two years to get to that point. The better part of one of those two years was devoted to searching for a developer who would restore the old buildings, someone who could make use of the federal grant money. No luck, as it turned out. There were a few nibbles and one bite, but no one took the hook. It wasn't even a project of mine—I got it as a political inheritance after H. died and S. left office. When it was clear that no one wanted to use the buildings, I made a particular point of consulting with the president of the preservation society, walking the area with him, coming to what I had thought was an agreeable understanding: some of the buildings might be saved, but most of them would have to go. The newspaper gave regular coverage to the project and no one reacted in an unusual way, so we thought it would be relatively smooth sailing. The new president of the preservation society changed all that.

A pale, intense young matron, she had come from one of the coastal cities further south where there had been extensive and successful preservation efforts. The wife of a top executive of a downtown business ("Is XYZ, Inc. really backing this?"), she launched a campaign that lasted for months, delayed construction, added to the cost of the project, and left a residue of bitterness. The new president must have put all her energy into the effort to save the buildings. She had no plan of what to do with them, no serious calculation of the costs of making them usable for large numbers of the public, just a straight-out plea for preservation, pure and simple. The people and groups she rallied went through the drill that is supposed to get the government mechanism to do what you want it to: publicity in the news media (they will cover a fight, if little else), appearances before the council and the relevant committees, calls on the city staff working on the project, and—in the beginning, at least—"one-on-ones" with council members.

When the project kept moving along in spite of the sentiments, they made appeals to federal and state preservation agencies, though none of the buildings had been entered on any historic register. That didn't generate any authoritative action, but we did get some angry letters on state government letterheads. Aesthetically, the most that could be said for the buildings was that they looked like something out of an Edward Hopper painting, but the negative publicity and some of the lobbying started to make a few council members nervous. So, it helped when the downtown business association (made up of people and businesses with real financial stakes in what happened) made vehement public statements in favor of the project. With governmental resolve shored up, the project continued.

The preservationists must have felt driven to desperation when they hit on their last major move. It took some doing for them to go to what was an unusual place for the upper crust to look for help, but I wonder if once they made the decision they didn't have an anticipation of triumph. No more gentility, no more working through channels. Instead, they would go for direct, highly publicized, popular pressure. It must have been Q. who had dreamed it up, since he suddenly took a prominent role in the struggle. It had to have been his idea, this abrupt inspiration of where the sheer force was located that could once and for all make the stubborn bastards on council and in the creaking juggernaut of city government do what the preservationists wanted done. In the world of power-as-a-thing-owned-by-individuals, they would go to the one man in town who really did "have" it, a guy who had not only been listed in the newspaper as being among the ten most powerful local people, but had also been listed as being among the most powerful figures nationally—our locally based but widely celebrated television evangelist. Before, they had been fooling around with tactical small potatoes—a verbal crossfire here, a few rhetorical grenades there. But that was all over. Now, they were going to go strategic. . . . No, they were going nuclear. They were going to drop Hill City's atomic bomb.

At one of the big church's Sunday services (not the televised one, though), Q. was given the pulpit and allowed to plea to the assembled faithful for their support for historic preservation. Petitions were printed up for people to sign, not addressing the market project but just old buildings in general. One of the younger members of the preacher's "inner circle" took a special interest in it and announced that "three to five thousand signatures" would be collected. He had the courtesy to call me on the telephone, introduce himself, and outline their plans. I thought it best to be blunt about it, and asked, "Is this an effort to block the market project?" He was blessedly candid: "Yes." And he was also blessedly willing to actually listen to the answers I gave to his questions. So we proceeded to discuss it all—the real costs of effective preservation, the problems that would be created if the devotees of preservation succeeded in getting boutiques to locate in some of the empty buildings that were next to still-functioning heavy industry, the large amounts of money that the city had already spent, and on and on. It lasted almost two hours. It was a distinct relief to deal with someone willing to think in terms of what could be done, really done, rather than just going for attention-grabbing rhetoric. We went through the history of the project, the progress of the controversy, the design process. When we finally exhausted the topic, he excused himself, and the conversation was over.

A couple of weeks later, he and an associate came to a regularly scheduled council meeting and made a brief, formal presentation of the petitions with "three thousand to five thousand" signatures on them. There was nothing more—no crowd, no heated pleas, no massive exercise of power, no TV campaign. They were low-key and correct, presented the stack of petitions to the clerk, and that was that. The preservationist group didn't even show up, but more argument wouldn't have accomplished much anyway. On order from city hall, the contractor's crew had started work early on a cool, gray morning two weeks earlier, toppling facades and pushing in walls with a big front-end loader. Whatever might come later, this project would go forward, and Hill City's atomic bomb wouldn't go off.

As an afterthought, I asked the clerk to count the number of signatures, excluding ones of out-of-towners and of students at the Bible college. The number of local signatures, citizens who wanted to involve themselves in a local activity, was only 282. This from a church audience that numbered in the thousands. "Should we leak it to the press?" I asked the clerk. To her credit she said nothing, just looked at me with a slight smile but no enthusiasm on her face. I answered myself: "Nah. The younger one was decent enough to find out some facts before he went out on a limb even further. Leave it." The paper dutifully reported the claims of "three to five thousand" signatures without, as usual, doing any double-checking. It would have been fun to embarrass them as well as those who had raised the clamor, but it wouldn't have accomplished anything. The bitterness the preservation group president had caused died out anyway, as what had been controversial became successful—once the market opened, there were more producers selling, more customers buying, and lots of public praise. From the city department head in charge: "We've got twice as many producers selling as last year, and on the Fourth of July three thousand people came! No kidding, we had men counting!"

What is the lesson in all this? Surely if power is something that can be possessed by individuals and can cause things to happen in a predetermined way, it should be possible to work it the other way—to look at what happens and then trace it back to the power that caused it. What lesson does that underscore—only that you can't fight city hall? But city hall can and does change its course of action. It (we?) hadn't changed course in this case, so perhaps the lesson is more subtle. Could it be that power consists of doing your homework and not losing your cool? That's not a dramatically compelling lesson. Perhaps it is something deeper, something that can take notice of how mismatched a rivalry can be between daydreams and nostalgia, on the one hand, and a concrete, positive course of action joined with the physical means to carry it out on the other—"Nothing will come from nothing."

Certainly city hall can pursue fantasies and come up with nothing. I hadn't remembered hearing about the Great Treasure Hunt, but there was Y., telling me about it. "Remember when you turned down the request to dig for the Everett Treasure at Artillery Park?" he asked. He had a big grin on his face, so I knew it couldn't have been serious business, but I couldn't remember the dig at all. He patiently reminded me, and then it came back. A retired army colonel and a retired CIA agent had claimed to have broken the famous three-part code that identified where a treasure, estimated to be worth "over $5 million dollars in today's currency," was buried. As it turned out, the treasure was supposedly under a prominent city landmark. Never mind that the whole thing was most likely a barroom joke from the 1820s, the age of American hyperbole. Two retired hotshots, residents of the Gulf coast, had doped it out. In committee we rejected it out of hand as pure silliness, the oldest infantile daydream in the world: buried treasure, findable by those who had secret knowledge of an esoteric code. It was all revealed to us in a personally typed, "confidential" letter: "You see I have broken the previously unbroken two codes. No. 2 was broken long ago that told what was buried. No. 1 told where it was buried (. . . only an empty hole remains). No. 3 was claimed to reveal the names and addresses of the 30 men in the Everett party. This did not prove out in the decoding. . . ."

And so on. Never mind that the new location didn't exist when the famous cipher was written, or that a generation had lapsed between the time of the original alleged burial and the alleged reburial. The basic legend was preposterous anyway. It told of a party going to the Southwest in 1819 and returning with a wagonload of gold and jewels, only to bury them. The whole story was probably a new joke on top of an old joke. I had wondered at the time why the staff even bothered to bring it to us.

Y. retrieved the correspondence on the matter—careful records and filing serve all kinds of purposes. When the treasure hunters had made their original contact with the city, the staff encouraged them: "At the present time, it seems that your request will be granted. The City Manager desires to discuss this request with the City Council. . . ." The expectation that permission would be granted came from the administrative memory that fifteen years before a similar request had been made and council had jumped at the opportunity to cash in on the treasure: "Should the treasure be found, Hill City will receive 50% of whatever the treasure may be worth. It seems that B., when he was City Manager, worked out such a similar deal."

I got a copy of the old contract that had been agreed to by the city government and by a treasure hunter from Chicago. It was explained in nice, legal language how the dig would be done, how the treasure would be split, and who would have custody of it. It was fascinating.

Y. went on to add: "That's when R. was on council; he took movies of it"—a story which turned out to be true. R., now a state legislator—always cool, somewhat aloof—cracked a smile, then a big grin, when I asked him about it at a get-together for another matter: "It was the funniest thing I've ever seen in all my years in public life. . . ." He told his version of it. Before the actual dig, the council had met in executive session to discuss what to do with the sudden great wealth that was about to come to the city. C., a respected professional man, argued vigorously and acrimoniously that such valuables should be put in a museum, where they could be seen by the public and serve as a tourist attraction. W., a successful businessman with a deserved reputation for being hardheaded and realistic, argued with considerable heat that the city's 50 percent share should be liquidated, and the revenue used to offset taxes. The arguments were lengthy. On the day designated in the contract, the council, the city manager, and the treasure hunter assembled secretly at dawn in Artillery Park. Spring mists were still hanging over the trees and the secretive little group. The digging began—mostly dirt, some pieces of scrap metal, a bone from a cow. As the sun rose and the mists burned away and the heap of dirt grew higher, the group slipped away, one by one. There was no treasure, of course. R. laughed again. (The second laugh in the same conversation—he really must have been tickled by it all.) I resisted the impulse to ask to see the film; it was probably more fun to imagine it anyway.

Where was the power in that episode? Where was the grandeur of public authority? A dozen or so foolish men, catching themselves before anyone else caught them in the oldest fantasy of all—the dream of sudden great wealth, release from the constraints of daily work and the prosaic, a leap into a brave new world. There was no power at all in that. Small wonder that very few people knew about the old flirtation with finding the famous treasure; small wonder that the petitioners we rejected had themselves insisted on secrecy ("As this subject matter is confidential, public exposure would result in a likely mob in the area . . ."). There was something practical in the request for secrecy—a large crowd can do damage—but it's hard to resist concluding that something more was at stake, that at bottom those caught up in the foolish daydream could still grasp that to dig and not uncover the treasure would be a very bad thing indeed. If all the king's horses and all the king's men couldn't reassemble Humpty-Dumpty, then there was not much chance that city hall, no matter how dignified and self-conscious of its status, could create a treasure where none existed. (But why worry? If a poll can reveal one "has" power, why should a communal laugh on a spring morning make any difference? Unless, of course, it was never something you "had," but was rather something attributed to you, something that could be easily taken away by the ones doing the attributing.) For all involved, did there remain an understanding that being caught up in a wild goose chase is far from demonstrating that one "has" power, but is instead a demonstration that one cannot "have" it, because whatever power is, it demands that you be decisively in touch with the real world?

What if power is not something in itself, but has meaning only as it describes the relationships of other things and makes no sense apart from them? We are comfortable talking about speed, in the sense of velocity. But there is no velocity in itself; it makes sense only as an expression of something that is moving in relation to something else. And if power is somehow more like that, then there are no simple if-then calculations. It is more like a game—not in any sense of idle play or lack of commitment to the outcome, but because it is moving, fluid, and requires a constant willingness to rethink what was taken for granted. It is not a hospitable environment for rigid thinking or a simple playing of the odds.

Maybe that's why the armchair types are so pathetic. They want to think that politics has got to be like blackjack, with betting "right" being just a matter of counting cards and remembering the chances—the one way to win. The result is that they are blind to how contingent, how circumstantial, politics can be. They are blind to how even those intimately involved can't trace out a chain of causes and how—despite the absence of defined, identified sequences of causes—you still have to work through plans and purposes to accomplish something, all the while with the thought in the back of your head that what you're trying may not work, that you may have to change and try something else.

If, as some suggest, politics is like a game, then it is like high-low poker, where the low and high hands split the pot. Or maybe it is like the seven-card version, where most of the cards are up, you bet on each card, and the last one dictates whether you go high for the A–2–3–4–5 straight or low for the 6–4–3–2–A bust. Maybe that doesn't settle it, because you've got to guess who else around the table is going high or low, since there's not just one direction—the others may not be doing what you're doing, they may be doing something quite different. In high-low you not only have to count cards and play the odds, you have to guess what the others are doing, and finally make a firm, no-going-back-on-it decision that you'll go one way or the other. Unless, of course, you fold. ("Three pair—damn. No one can do anything with three goddamn pair!")

Like games and gambling, it takes some zest for the action, some passion for the involvement itself, to stay with it and make up for the inevitable losses. In the short run, it doesn't even make a lot of difference where the passion comes from—ego, greed, fear, the exhilaration of an absorbing commitment. Empires are conquered, canals are dug, regulations are posted and enforced, and bulldozers are directed to move only if somebody does it. If nobody acts, nothing will happen, no matter how much something is wished for, wanted, or needed. If there is nothing there, no object but just dreams of buried treasure or unanchored nostalgia, then equally, nothing happens. It should take neither great intelligence nor elaborate education to recognize this. Perhaps it is enough to be aware of the truth that Shakespeare put in the mouth of futile, doomed Lear: "Nothing will come from nothing."

But street talk's definition of power has some real value, anyway. In addition to being a source of error, it is an irreplaceable monument to the ancient ineradicable fear, the dread of power that the other has (or may have) over us in the primordial game of combat. So, one more set of images in yet another place.

This time, C. and I found it easier just to leave the others in town so they could plan the next outing while we indulged in C.'s hobby, archaeology—an eccentricity for most of the others, or at least not amusing enough to pursue in the sultry heat that had settled in a haze over the Bavarian countryside. At a couple of places on the hillsides (the Teutons thought it best to seek security on the high ground), we found a few pottery fragments. The last visit would be to the foundations of a *ritter schloss,* a "knight's castle," which is to say a barbarian fortress and palisade from the inchoate, unrecorded disorder of the Dark Ages. We drove up a winding country lane, up a valley toward some hills, and parked in the shade of the trees at a trout pond. The local people who tended the pond had built a little shack and kept a fireplace—a quiet, rural refuge for an evening's fish fry? We poked around, then started up the hillside which the government had carefully and meticulously reforested with regular plantings of fir trees. They had grown tall, and we struggled upward in the shadowy gloom created by their interlocking branches. No underbrush grew beneath the trees, and there were few low branches—just the straight columns of the trunks, the dark green canopy high above, and the dry summer heat. The dead needles were so thick on the ground that they spilled into our shoes; there was no sound but our own puffing. Then, as we rounded the side of the hill, still in the shade, the great, geometrical slopes of the fortification ditch loomed in front of us, straight and smooth and strangely punctuated by the tree trunks still planted at the same intervals as the rest of the forest. We clambered down into the ditch, as much for the relief of taking a few downhill steps as anything else. C. found a small metal sign, erected by the appropriate agency, that estimated a possible age for the earthworks, accurate to within a century or two, and told us that *wenig,* very little, was known about whatever willful Germanic chieftain built his stronghold here. *Wenig,* indeed—nameless, voiceless, lost to memory and recollection. He must have driven his slaves or serfs or retainers hard to move and pack so much dirt and to establish himself on this vantage point over the flat, fertile valley. Were any battles fought here, with the women and children cowering inside the rough, dark fortress, their pale, oval faces even paler as they listened to the curses, the shouted commands, the shrieks outside?

Just then, as we stood in fatigued silence, the air above us cracked with the whining roar of a fighter jet, and then, right behind it, another. The noise reverberated for a few seconds, then died in its own echo. C. turned to me, "Ours."

From over a decade's intelligence work in Germany he knew American combat aircraft when he heard them. I murmured something in response as we both pondered the peculiar juxtaposition of two varieties of primal power, fifteen hundred years apart. The two powers were joined in their sense of the need to be ready to fight the other: the unknown, willful chieftan, hacking out some safety for himself and his people in a chaos that would otherwise swallow them, and, just above us, the anonymous pilots of "ours," doing something not very different from the watchmen who once guarded the palisade of this primitive fortress, living through the old nighttime wariness.

Still, we do not live in a wilderness or a war zone. Our city is mostly quiet at night. So we ought to digress from street talk's glib primitivism in matters of power to some farther-reaching, more elaborate and extended understanding of how energy is channeled to a community and an act— not just an act as a unit in response to a sudden crisis or outcry, but an act that occurs in known, predictable ways—an act that uses its public institutions to do public things and to talk about them. Limited though it is, perhaps we ought to have recourse to our century's understanding of "the power," our century's source of energy for domestic improvement and convenience, electricity. "The power," alternating electric current that is nothing in itself (don't protest—remember the old joke on the youngster new on the job: "Hey, buddy. Run over to the storeroom and get us a bucket of kilowatts") but becomes amazing energy when the right things are set in the correct relation to each other. Channeled and contained, consciously directed with the proper skill, it becomes light, warmth, and effort. Perhaps for a community to "have power," it is most important to set its pathways and uses, to acknowledge that nothing that requires it will work without it, and that it must be used with modesty and care.

SIX

•

Meetings

I am born into a world which is inhabited by those
who will confront me.

—Alfred Schutz, "Dimensions of the Social World"

The meetings blur together. After a few days they lose whatever distinctive features they had and fade into nothing but more entries on the perpetually lengthening list in the pocket calendar I try to keep. Times, places, dates, names—all entered in roughly the same way (those that actually do get entered) regardless of the occasion's importance or lack of it. Face after face, room after room, the personalities, anxieties, and settings, in all their complexity, are squeezed into the pale green boxes on the pocket calendar.

Calendars and clocks: in alliance with the telephone, they shape my day. Or rather they disintegrate it first and then reshape it, grinding the irregular grains of living into the uniform flour of the calendar, squeezing them into regular little loaves of times, places, dates, and names. I keep the calendars of years past in the tidy file boxes they came in, as if they mattered. The net result is that the dust slowly accumulates on the boxes rather than the monthly booklets themselves.

Meeting after meeting, flicking past my awareness in accelerating succession, like telephone poles seen from a bus window, finally reaching some terminal velocity of habit and sheer endurance. Can this blur of meetings be sorted out, given some explicit coherence, reduced to a manageable technique and thus become "no big deal"? Maybe I should stop worrying about the other parts and just attend to what's external and observable.

I'll start with the behaviorally simplest of meetings—almost, indeed, a nonmeeting—the telephone call. Note two calls, "a" and "b," of yesterday, thus: alone in room and plastic apparatus buzzes; pick up semiattached piece of apparatus and place to mouth and ear; emit noises at intervals, replace piece on apparatus, and fall silent.

Hmmm. Not much so far. Maybe we need more observation and measurement; maybe we need to be stricter in the interest of science. OK. We additionally note that call "a" took twenty minutes of time and that I remained seated. By contrast, scientifically observed call "b" was performed from a standing position and lasted only three minutes. We note that call "a" lasted almost seven times as long as call "b." Several more calls and perhaps we could plot the different times, on arithmetical or logarithmic coordinates, to explore the relationship of their length magnitudes. In the meantime, we can puzzle over the sitting/standing dichotomy. Later, with more data, we will know whether "a" is several orders of magnitude greater than "b," or if it is a mere baby step above.

While the data accumulates on phone calls, we can move on to those meetings that are more complex—polycentric meetings with more than one participant. With their richer efflorescence of overt behaviors, surely there is light there to be shed on the principal question. Consider meeting "c" this week: enter building, ride elevator to one of the floors, enter room, emit noises at seated female, stand and look at pictures on wall. Phase two of meeting: B. and D. emerge from another room, all present make primate submission gestures and clasp right hands, proving that there are no weapons in them. Move to another room, emit noises, repeat gestures and repeat demonstration of absence of weapons in right hands (boot knives, pistols in shoulder holsters, and weapons in the form of bank accounts are not covered by these customs). Take seats around tables. Emit noises at intervals. P. (finally) comes in—repeat gestures, and so on. All emit noises identical to those emitted before P. arrived. Note that P. is taller, wears darker suit and more somber silk tie than the others. Everyone emits exactly the same noises for the third time, but in a different order. All stare at ceiling, then at each other. Emit noises fourth time. P. moves lips somewhat differently, so as to expose teeth fully and emit staccato, barking noise. All repeat P.'s expression, stand and emit noises, and prove a final time that certain customary implements of violence are not at hand. Ride the elevator down to the first floor and go out on the sidewalk. End of meeting "c."

Well, that is obviously a complex phenomenon, verifiably akin to meeting "d" held earlier in the week: meet a male and a female at large front door of building, ride elevator up, go to room where we drink cups of brown liquid, emit noises, make primate submission gestures, sit around table and emit noises, and so on.

Both "c" and "d" lasted about forty-five minutes. Could this be a pattern worthy of attention as a nomothetic regularity? But to pursue this line of reasoning, it would be necessary to account for the apparent anomaly of meeting "e," held the week before in a car, in the rain, in front of a restaurant that turned out to be closed on Mondays. This one lasts only twenty minutes, raising an obvious question: Are meetings held in cars in the rain regularly half the length of meetings held around tables in buildings? It would be interesting to know, for those of us who would like to save time.

Apparently, a second stage of the research agenda demands our attention. Does the sitting/standing–phone-call dichotomy share a relationship with the meetings-in-rooms/meetings-in-cars dichotomy? If so, it may be possible to lay the groundwork for a general theory of meetings, possibly even develop some practical applications. If I want to cut down on the amount of time I spend in meetings, should I schedule more meetings in cars? ("Hi. Let's get together in the parking lot at the mall. I'll be in the blue Chevy under the department store sign. . . .") Or maybe they would be even shorter if I put a cellular phone in the car to call other people in their cars, if they have cellular phones too. . . .

Does reducing the meetings to their externals make it any easier? Is "planning your work and working your plan" really a substitute for being so immersed in the activity that personalities, events, projects, resources, and language are no longer separate, but become a lived network of what is to be done? The paradox is that describing meetings in terms of the "doings" doesn't get us very close to actual practice, to what one has to *do*. Maybe words are the problem. After all, meetings aren't the activities themselves; they're talk and writing about activities. Maybe the key is the use of words and language.

Take, for example, meeting "f," held this week. It had something as yet unmentioned, a written agenda, and it lasted three hours, so maybe there's another dichotomy—meetings with written words and meetings without. The group coming to this meeting with a gaggle of city officials was one of the groups working for the preservation of old buildings. This time the building was an old theater. A triumph in the days of vaudeville, it was later used as a movie theater. The group had wanted to bring it back to its original use, but without much luck. . . . But no, we're not supposed to talk about context and identities and all that. Instead, let's look at how those at the meeting used signs and symbols that "stand for" things in the real world and see if that doesn't straighten things out.

Building stands for the building itself, a slowly decaying hulk that is almost alone in being the only undemolished or unrestored old structure at its end of Main Street. It had been unoccupied for years. The next major written symbols are the dollar signs and numbers that stand for money, but not enough money. The group hadn't been able to raise what it needed to restore the building, not to mention provide an endowment for its operation as a legitimate theater. But the stated (in words!) purpose of the meeting was to transfer a small amount of federal grant money that had been earmarked for construction work to another purpose—the purchase from the city of the smallish, worn, brick building next to the theater. In its last life it had been an auto-glass and upholstery shop, and because of that it was now grandiosely referred to as "The E. Building" in the documents. We explicitly agreed, in black and white. They would take possession of the building and use an amount that would be left over to clean up the front of it.

Now, let's try some of the accompanying spoken language: "There's really no need to cut a check for the purchase of the building—we can just do an in-house transfer and deed it over." Y., their perpetually suspicious executive director, looked apprehensive again; he calmed down when he saw the members of his board nod assent. "Then we'll just write a check for the remainder, and you-all can get to work on the front." The semiotic stew now seems to be thickening a little. Part of the expressed amount of money turns out not to stand for money, after all, but for a bookkeeping operation—signs standing for a manipulation of signs. (Of course, we won't count Y.'s "body language" as he twisted in his chair, his eyes darting, his uncommonly large nostrils flaring—like a wild animal out of its habitat and afraid.)

Next, as I had been blessedly forewarned, came the rest of what they were there for—the really big question that brought into the discussion implications of things far beyond the building and the arrangements for its preservation, the question that would additionally bring in such arcane issues as the city's debt structure and public opinion about people and things having no apparent relation to the matter explicitly before us: "Would the city take over the entire project?" It was a short enough question, but its implications stretched on and on for anyone who had been involved in the matter over a period of years—implications that went beyond the obvious, easily stated goals of the people who had gotten themselves involved in the original movement to keep the building from being torn down. For one thing, the request flew in the face of the history of the movement, which had assured city hall and the public for years that the renovations would be accomplished with private funds, that there would be no request for local government funds (the entire project had been estimated to cost an amount equal to fifty dollars for every man, woman, and child in the city). For another thing, the responsibilities that would inevitably follow the city's taking it over—paying for maintenance of the restoration, managing the building, doing what would be necessary to put the building to use so that it would generate some income—were left wholly undiscussed, probably because any address to them would shatter whatever semblance of reasonability the request might appear to have. And what about the impact on the local theater group that was struggling to support its own facility? And so on.

In addition, street talk had even identified a probable purchaser. So, if the words at wordy meetings like this one are indeed nothing more than little signs that simply substitute for a reality that they unambiguously point to, why ask if the city would take it all over? In the circumstances of this particular meeting, the answer was simple enough. K. had been the one identified as the potential purchaser, and he would be unpopular with most of the people who had donated money and effort to the project. So, for the directors who had come to the understanding that they had to get it off their hands, what better way to cover their (impolite portion of anatomy) than to get the city to turn it down, explicitly, and at this particular time? If someone were to complain, it would be an easy matter to just point the finger: "Well, we asked the city to take it, and they turned it down. . . ." That was fair enough. The city could be the fall guy—the price of leadership and all that. Besides, if K. did take it, the city would be off the hook—if he did something with it.

But the words—what do we make of the analysis of words when they are used as smokescreens, standing for something other than what they point to? What do we do when words turn out to be more like curtains that change their transparency as the breeze turns them this way and that? What happens to the effort to be strictly rational? Some of the critically important words are, indeed, explicit and direct. But still others are indirect and evasive, suggesting and then withdrawing the suggestion, so that the group's attention comes to rest on something else entirely. And if that isn't enough, what can be made of words that become important in themselves? Words can be therapeutic incantations whose resonances generate inner comfort. Consider the words of a representative of group V, invited to speak at a regular council meeting: "We are not going to be ignored any more!" This concluding outburst came after a private group and some city officials—who had assured group V that it would be welcome—spent the preceding fifteen minutes providing recognition for group V, as well as the members of groups W and X. Groups W and X had, in fact, been waiting much longer. No one on the council batted an eye. Groups always behave that way, and it's better to just let them "ventilate." Not doing so had been the source of D.'s downfall and S.'s unpopularity, and no one wants to follow the pattern of their political careers—sudden ascendancy and equally sudden demise.

So much, then, for the laboratory effort. To talk about meetings it is necessary to return to the original plan, to try to examine the events themselves, to become abnormally aware of my own perceptions of them, and to give the account in those terms. Therefore, I must try to reconstruct how meetings present themselves. I must remind myself that they are encounters, problematic juxtapositions that always raise an inner reflex of anxiety: How do I look? What will they think? Will it turn out well? But reflection can be an enemy. It's better to plunge in and not worry about whether I've been the presumptuous, disruptive element one more time. As strange as the sheer external record of meetings can look, there are stranger things yet.

For example, some meetings are not actual meetings at all. What's the proper reaction when someone comes up and says, with a lift in the voice and a brighter-than-usual smile, "I saw you on TV last night"? They may have seen my image on their sets, but I certainly didn't see them. We all know what the mass media is, so I shouldn't expect a different behavior from others, but my inner reaction is always the same: a quick spasm of annoyance. Why should I feel such a thing when the person is clearly trying to be friendly, to make a passing acknowledgment of my official position in an appropriately light way? I certainly can't say what I momentarily feel: "You didn't see *me*. You saw a bunch of photons chasing around a cathode ray tube!" No. I just smile, maybe tease them about having nothing better to do then park themselves in front of the tube. Yet I can't free myself of a worry. They think they know *me* because of that; they think we met when I saw nothing but the vacant glass eye of the camera and the little bright red light that said that the camera was on. It was not a meeting at all, but at best a demimeeting, the shadow of an encounter.

It's easier to know what to make of the ones that are explicitly tied to the office. Responding to a request for an official visit to a growing professional firm: "Look, I'll be downtown first thing in the morning, anyway. What if I just came by your place? What time do you get in?" This had grown out of some casual conversation at another meeting—a planned meeting growing out of a small unplanned one that was part of a larger, very planned meeting that was addressing a different matter entirely. It's not that the inviter didn't have an agenda of his own that he was pursuing in an appropriately low-key way—he wanted money for downtown rehabilitation. Though his project fully qualified, he evidently thought it best to "touch base" to keep everything on track.

For me, the explicit public meetings are easier—real gatherings of real people for overt political purposes. Yet, for a lot of people, speaking at a public meeting is a feat they wouldn't dare try: "I don't see how you do it. I hate standing up in front of an audience." My only response is to murmur something about not minding it—there's no point in explaining that meetings are easy for me, that they are actually enjoyable because they are a little exciting.

So, it's easy to commit to a speaking engagement, especially one that's a month or more away—the further off the date, the easier it is to make the commitment. Only when the date begins to close in (the tyranny of the calendar) do I start to fret: "Damn, there's enough to do already that actually *has* to be done. . . . Will anyone be paying attention to the information anyway?" But enough internal griping—I make sure I've got a second clean shirt for the day, have a second shave that night, wolf dinner down, and bolt out the door for yet another 7:30 P.M. meeting. . . .

One such meeting took place at a church-sponsored women's club. There was little enough pressure: I could choose my own topic and they had no axes to grind—probably just wanted to do some sizing-up and maybe get the sense that they could contact city hall readily if they needed to. Since the group was part of a fundamentalist church that ran its own school system, the meeting was held in the boardroom of a building that housed school activities as well as church operations. There was a nice table, comfortable chairs, tasteful decor, and an audience of about twenty. It was genteel enough, though somewhere else in the same building the high school's basketball team was playing the team from a school for the deaf. The smell of popcorn filled the corridors, and even in our room we could hear the occasional crescendos of squeals and shouting from the spectators. The team for the deaf school got their signals from a deep bass drum—evidently a big one, since its tones resonated through the gym floor and through the structure of the building itself. It was more tangible than audible, shaking our room and its furniture ever so slightly at each beat.

It all served to remind me that whatever I had to say wouldn't be important to very many people, that even in this building there were more human souls who were a lot more excited about basketball than these women were about me. Chastened, I began to address the twenty or so mostly pleasant, pale, round faces ringed around the dark, polished wood of the table top. The meeting began with a devotion, given by a young matron with an exceptionally attractive face—strong, regular features with a sculptured delicacy about them and large, blue eyes, luminous with equal parts of religiosity and illness. She spoke of trying to understand God's purpose in times of sickness, her body flaccid and at ease only when slumped in the chair.

I gave them the standard speech on government's problems—too large, too expensive, too self-obsessed to be self-disciplined—a message with which they would be comfortable. I kept it general—the practical complexities of actually working toward some sort of Jeffersonian ideal are not matters with which most self-styled Jeffersonians are much interested. The group seemed to like eye contact, so I laid on the eye contact, looking each one in the eyes. After one declaration about inefficiency, I caught an affirmative nod, so I stepped up the tempo. Maybe I was really connecting! I turned my head again and caught another affirmative nod from the same woman—she seemed really excited. I looked back to her again: same smile, same nod. Then, said silently to myself: "Damn!" I'd been taking cues from a "nodder." She'd have that grin and that up-and-down bob of her head for anyone and anything. She'd have smiled and nodded if I suggested the reintroduction of typhoid fever or the abolition of frozen food. I had almost made a fool of myself again, misled by the eternal wish to be a hero. Humbled, I went back to my scribbled notes.

With the formal speech finished, it was time for question and answer. There were a couple of general ones—cliché trading—but then the women moved to the particular. One asked a specific question about a parking ordinance that the council had enacted, at my insistence and over the city manager's mild objection and the police chief's protest. The ordinance would affect their church's overflow parking, no doubt, though it was far from being aimed at them. The questioner was trying to discover hostile intent—as usual, the ever-popular paranoia about public things. Happily, the preacher's wife intervened: "J. says it's fair." They relaxed; I fielded some nice questions about future ambitions, then the discussion was over and I joined them for refreshments. It was difficult to circulate, so I didn't. (Was I being deferential to perceived shyness in them, or was I just being timid and lazy?) I had a pleasant chat with the program chairwoman, a small, lively woman who looked like she would have been more at home in casual clothes. She offered a small honorarium. I refused; she insisted. Oh well, why not? I accepted. It would buy a dinner out. With the meeting over, I found my way down the corridor, through the popcorn smells and the vibrations from the still-throbbing drum, and out into a cold, clear night. There was time enough left in the evening to get some work done before bedtime—not always the case with evening civic speeches.

But that kind of occasion, the formal talk to an identifiable group, is not really very political, no matter what people think. It may be the stereotype that shows up on TV and in bad movies, but the vision of the Honorable M., stylish in a dark-blue power suit and orating to an adoring audience, conveys nothing about politics and real meetings. It doesn't even convey much about what the formal talk is—political theater. And even as theater, it's frequently stylized and superficial, confined to the ritual itera-tion of already-known lines by already-known characters, sort of a political Kabuki. The audience does not come to learn or to be informed; it is there to critique the set performance and be amazed that those who choose to be actors would drop the spontaneity of natural existence and live in the impossibly artificial world of the performance.

Some seem never to make it back to the natural world. D. and I were at a civic-club dinner in Valley City once and happened to sit with one of their elected officials. He was young, impeccably dressed, and traded clichés with us without missing a beat. The proceedings began, clumsy and poorly organized. Out of politeness, we had stopped talking, but our table companion went further than that. The moment the program began, he snapped around in his chair to face the head table and froze into a pose. He crossed his legs and clasped his hands firmly on his upper knee. He held his back straight, tilted his chin slightly upward, and a faint smile froze on his face. Once in position he didn't budge. His only expression was one of rapt attention. Lord only knows what was going on inside his head; he had petrified for the duration.

It was D.'s reaction that struck me, not the posing. D. had just watched him at first without anything registering; then, something hit him—some understanding that the pose was part of something more comprehensive. In a stage whisper, D. blurted at me: "He's stone political!" He didn't stop there; whatever the insight was that had come to him took over his entire being: "I can't believe it—the guy's stone political!" It was louder the second time; the official wasn't more than ten feet away and the noise from the front of the room surely wasn't enough to drown D. out. I tried to shush him, but he wouldn't do more than drop his voice a notch: "This is unreal! I can't believe it. . . . Stone political!" If the official ever heard any of D.'s outbursts, he didn't show it. He just kept the same position, with a faint smile on his face, a blissful countenance, a marvel of civic performance.

In D.'s view, our table companion had somehow found a way to achieve the complete denial of spontaneous human interaction. He had come to the point where his life was absorbed in the studied fulfillment of a preconceived notion of his public role. D.'s amazement at discovering someone who could actually do this was accurate enough, but I couldn't help but be alarmed at how loudly he announced it. And, deep down, I couldn't keep from resenting the way he used the word "political" to describe it. I felt, but never said, that it wasn't political at all. It had nothing, or at least very little, to do with politics or policy or how we achieve a polity. It may in fact be necessary to look respectable in public and to not allow gossip about an individual officeholder to overwhelm what should (and, often enough, doesn't) take place: the discussion of the public consequences of what the official does.

If meetings are not the schedule of confrontations, even though they necessarily involve carefully kept schedules, neither are they theatrical performances, even though they necessarily involve some theatrics. At bottom, meetings are something else, something that is either fulfilled or not, something qualitative. Otherwise, the question that is always asked wouldn't make the sense it always does: "D'ya think it was a good meeting?" Generally, the person asking the question thinks it was, hoping for the answer: "Yeah. I think it was." It's only asked about good meetings because bad meetings aren't meetings, they're wastes of time—not "somethings" but rather "nothings." They are only confusion, disorder, and emotional energy drained with nothing to show for it, nothing established or resolved, nothing brought into being.

Shouldn't it be regarded as disturbing that so many people think of public meetings strictly as spectator events, where the few perform for the many? Certainly, they're not considered something that ordinary citizens take part in as a matter of practical government. Consider the elderly woman who came up to me after a campaign rally where I had given a pep talk for one of the candidates. She was shy and deferential and seemed to be glad that her grown daughter was with her. She asked if I remembered her from a public hearing that had been held a year or so before. "I'm not sure," I said, "Remind me. . . ." Her daughter spoke up at that point. For that formal public hearing on a rezoning matter, the woman had organized and led the hearing testimony from a neighborhood group. She had done well; her own statement had been direct and practical, and her group had spent most of their effort addressing the matter at hand, not trying to orate or call down the wrath of heaven. They had made sense and won their case. It had seemed so ordinary and obvious at the time that I had forgotten it. (Maybe that made us, the governing body, pretty good—we reacted to the tangible and the specific, not to rhetoric.) But what had seemed easy for her at that meeting hadn't been easy at all. She explained herself: "That was the first time I ever spoke at a public meeting. I didn't think I could do it. . . ." Well, I thought, I'll be damned; she had been nearly terrified and none of us knew it. "Oh, I remember. No, no need to worry. You did a good job. Clear and straightforward . . ." She was beaming; her smiling daughter took over: "I don't think she's ready to do it again anytime soon."

Maybe it's too easy for me to do the public speaking bit. I don't appreciate what stress is involved for others, especially for someone like that—someone who probably thought of herself as "not the kind of person who does that sort of thing." People imagine that they've got to put on a grand performance or else look like a fool. Really it's the opposite: the extent to which people avoid the temptation to use a public forum for a pulpit and instead stick to what they actually know something about is the measure of "effective public speaking." And it's not a matter of status or education. Just about everyone has something worth sharing, a perspective that is uniquely their own on something with which they are in touch. And by the same token, elaborate and sophisticated efforts to impress can become bizarre and otherworldly.

Take the second time in less than three years that we settled ourselves for a formal presentation by a nationally known group of architects and planners of a downtown renovation proposal. The plans and the planners had changed from the first time, but the room, the faces, and the mood of calm expectation were the same. There was an artist's easel up front to hold some of the drawings and maps; a slide projector and transparencies were ready to go. It was apparently intended to be a polished presentation. The sparse crowd composed itself. The members of the council were all attentive, the faces of the municipal staff that had nursed this group of consultants through this set of proposals were placid, the journalists were poised on the edge of boredom. The consultants were dressed in carefully dark suits, silk ties—serious men. The previous group of planners had radiated an air of seedy academicism; this bunch looked like they at least knew how to make money at what they were doing.

They began. The lights were out, the projector was on. A brief review of financial considerations was given to establish an air of reality about the proceedings, and pictures of the firm's past achievements were shown. Then, the projector was off, the lights were on. Maps of rerouted streets were provided, with both new and renovated buildings reduced to exact geometric shapes. There was a little sidestreet park (diagonally across from the building that the mayor had recently purchased—humph.) The drama was carefully built, the apostles of progress bringing enlightenment to the benighted. We were taken from the geometric abstractions of the map to the visually more helpful perspective sketches. There would be a new hotel/motel, a new office building, a new parking deck. "Questions? We want this to be a shirtsleeve session, gentlemen." The questions were predictable enough—the elected officials led off: What was this trapezoid? What was the size of that building? What were the limits of the convention facilities? The staff and finally even the reporters were drawn into the communion, fascinated by the vision of what might be: an alternate world.

There were clean, perfect buildings, gently curving streets, artfully placed and immaculately groomed shrubbery; a manageable number of brightly colored automobiles glided silently by on watercolor tires. There was no dialogue, no debate, no skirmishing among differing points of view. The infinite possibilities of the future were reduced to an architectural rendering that crystallized the vision of those in the room to the exclusion of any alternative. Feel the gentle spray of this fountain, spouting into the breezeless air of an everlasting spring morning. Greet these silent, faceless people, frozen in time so that we can inject ourselves into their world and withdraw at will. . . .

The staff were rapt; they were cherubim, attendant upon the seraphic consultants who had revealed this heavenly wonder. Even the reporters relented and let themselves become transported. For the moment, the entire group was frozen, as if for an old-fashioned *tableau vivant*. Were a local Rembrandt to paint a portrait of the city council, he could choose no better moment then this to commit to canvas. The council itself, seated behind the great, raised, judicial bench that dominates the chamber. Clustered before and below is the city staff; at the center, the consultant stands, a triumphant genius whose brilliance reflects honor and glory on these, his solid, attentive patrons, each caught in a characteristic pose.

Of course, the mood broke when someone asked how much it would actually cost the city. And the mood had been what the meeting was there to set—it was more a show than a meeting, a show that required the assent of the audience to have any effect. Part of the visionary project was finally built, but in a different style and configuration than had been shown, and it had a shaky financial footing.

It is curious that a meeting can be regarded as successful and still involve little more than an ordinary exchange of understandings. Just as curious is the fact that a sophisticated and elaborate presentation at a prestigious gathering can turn out to be not much of a meeting. And still the question is asked: "Was it a good meeting?" How many ways can the question be asked? Was it worth the time? Did you get anything done? Whatever the form, the question points to something other than efficiency (X meetings in Y amount of time); it certainly points to something other than political theater. Asked again, "Did you get anything done?" A good question, but an odd one. How can a meeting *do* something when everyone knows that a meeting is, by definition, not a doing at all, but something else, something that has to do with the time before there can be any doing. At the very most, all a meeting can reach is a decision—not the carrying out of a decision, just the decision itself. Or maybe what is reached is a decision not to do something, or, more subtly, finding out if someone else might or might not do something.

Years back, there was the last session of the old statewide city-county negotiating team. The short windows at the top of the room in the office building in Capitol City were too wide for us to see out, but they did let in the bright, late-morning sunlight. Across the front of the room, the brightly colored backs of the books set off the library/conference room's crisp, corporate-style decor. In front of the bookshelves were the three new and authoritative participants in the discussions we had been carrying on for some months. They were the ones at whom our efforts had been aimed—two key state legislators and the governor's chief administrative assistant. They were there to tell us what the chances of success would be for the proposal of our combined study group of city and county officials.

The study group had been assembled to look for ways to soften the bitter animosity between counties and cities that the state's annexation laws and financial aid formulas had created. For months we had met and negotiated, first in separate city and county caucuses, then together. The early sessions were held on carefully chosen neutral ground, such as hotel conference rooms. The group's confidence gradually rose to the point where the last meeting was able to be held, unself-consciously, in this, the city association's library/conference room. Fifteen members had come, all elected officials from their home jurisdictions, as well as the executive directors of both associations. After all that had gone before, the proposals were now leaving our hands. Attention was very firmly focused on the three men behind the table that had been set up in the front of the room.

The first to speak was B. Though no older than middle age, he was a senior legislator and chairman of the committee whose approval was absolutely necessary if our proposal was going to go anywhere at all. "Ladies and gentlemen, if you wanted something like this, you should have decided it some months ago." His plump face was a study in evenly tanned circles—rounded chin, small bulbous nose, pouting lips, and fleshy cheeks, which were shaking slightly with vehemence. His gray hair and perfectly tailored suit kept him from looking childlike. He continued, his unwelcome words falling on seventeen sets of astonished ears. The two executive directors, our respective full-time lobbyists and political operatives, were poker-faced, frozen and unreacting. Had they known earlier? The study-group members were less guarded. Some murmured audibly; others made faces—open-mouthed wonder, eyes rolled upward in mock appeal to heaven, and the like. B. had just cut the heart out of what we were trying to do. "Months earlier," he had said. Damn it, we had decided it months earlier! Or we thought we had. Damn, damn, damn. All that time, effort, and hope, down the drain.

M., the legislator we had been dealing with all along on this business, was slumped at the opposite end of the table from B. He looked pale, nervous, and was sporting a big razor nick under his lower lip. Damn *him*! He knew what we were doing and was supposedly passing it on. W., the governor's assistant, sat between M. and B., attired in a proper, executive, blue blazer and gray slacks, confident and enjoying the attention.

Our proposal had been simple. It recognized that cities annexed for economic reasons—if they added to their territories—could grow economically to meet the demands for expenditure that fall on aging cities, as well as make the newer developed area part of the body politic. Therefore, if the legislature was to continue its ban on annexation as the counties had requested, the affected cities should get appropriate compensation from the state. To make this palatable to the cities in the long run, the counties' representatives to the study group agreed that state aid should no longer disproportionately favor the counties. We had worked hard to get that far. M. had been told about the plan, and evidently had just sat on it. D. had once mentioned that his locality didn't gain anything under our proposal. Had he known this was coming and not told us? M. stayed silent. W. began to speak for the governor: "The governor's staff has reviewed the matter . . . [blah, blah] and feels that X million dollars will be available for the annexation compromise." Surprise! . . . No, not surprise: amazement and stupefaction. X was way *more* than we had wanted in our proposal. They wouldn't do what we suggested, but they were prepared to spend more money! W. went on: the governor and Appropriations Committee had agreed that X million would be available on a continuing basis, that it would be labeled "law enforcement assistance," that it would be available to all jurisdictions, and that the locality wouldn't be required to actually spend more money on law enforcement. In effect, they could spend the money on whatever they saw fit, which meant a small, regular dole to relieve some immediate fiscal pressure. But in the long run, it would change nothing, because the relations of cities and counties wouldn't be affected. "The governor wants you to understand that this is all that can be allocated on this matter." B. added: "Ladies and gentlemen, this is what will get through the assembly." In short, take it or leave it.

B. was good at his job, I'd give him credit for that—clear and direct, he knew what was going through our minds, and he answered our questions without ever having to hear us ask them. The only decision our committee had to make was whether we would take it and shut up or not. Of course, we took it. It's never a good idea to turn down money, especially since it was more than we asked for. But what we had tried to do would be lost, and the nagging question of what could be done about the basic structural problems of local government was shoved under the carpet one more time. The bill did pass, the money was appropriated, and the chief legislative sponsor of the measure was widely and approvingly quoted in the state papers, saying that the measure would simultaneously ease city/county tensions and improve law enforcement. We knew better, but everyone kept quiet. There was no sense in trying to explain how less could have been spent, how galling the structural problems were, and how refreshing it was for the principal antagonists to find enough common ground to start working together on something that involved enormous amounts of public money, the possibility of better communities, and a way to short-circuit petty wrangling.

The public doesn't care about matters of government that are so general they have to be expressed abstractly—not a fault, really. There are enough silly abstractions floating around that it doesn't seem fair to ask that people sort through them, address themselves to the ones that do make sense, and then let their opinions be known. It is up to those who do have an understanding of them to try to work things out so that govern-

ment becomes a little less absurd, a little more efficient, a little more hu-
mane. We had failed this time—or had the three at the front of the room?

Meetings are not just entries on calendars or ritual performances of
social courtesies or political theater. Meetings have to be an encounter
between those who will learn from each other, who have the capacity to do
something with what they learn, who can use the encounter to accomplish
some particular thing worth doing. All the grandiose political pronouncements, all the volumes of statistics, all the passionate representations of
what the people want, pale to insignificance and become no more than
background compared to the particulars of meetings: Who will actually
get together? What will they address? Can what they address actually be
dealt with by developing a better common understanding? What other
meetings are taking place? More subtly, those in the meeting must have the
capacity to carry out their portion of the common understanding once
they leave.

Meetings. So many that they do blur together. Some regularly scheduled and formal, others casual, even accidental. But even an accidental,
unplanned meeting can be suddenly deepened by personal impulse and
become the only way to find out what someone really thinks, what range
of possibilities they see. How does our cumbersome, incredibly complicated mechanism of government actually work? On the basis of meetings,
of course. Meetings running all the way from formal, legally prescribed
ones to happenstance contacts. One after another, different times, different
places. Crammed into days that are too short, making demands on attention that are almost impossible to meet. Still, even when fatigue sets in, it's
important to be "up" for them, to concentrate on whatever it is.

And I find myself wondering, why am I drawn to them?

SEVEN

•

Civis

The citizen . . . is best defined by the one criterion, "a man who shares in the administration of justice and the holding of office."
—Aristotle, *The Politics*

When you ask people when they feel like they've gotten to Hill City, you get a variety of answers: "On 99 north, when you get to the old Holiday Inn in Monroe Hills. What's it called now? . . ." "From Milltown, when I'm coming down that last hill before you can see all those little businesses near the road into the airport." "Out 110 east, when you see the insurance company sign, not when you see that city limits sign that's stuck way out in the country." Monroe Hills, of course, is outside the city limits, and so is the airport—it is owned by the city, but not legally *in* it. Oddly enough, the insurance company sign is well within the legal limits. For a while, we'll enjoy the rare luxury of having land that is not built-up actually inside the city limits. But the General Assembly will see that it doesn't happen again.

The city limits—artificial, arbitrary, and compelling. On the old bridge, the boundary is marked only by a little metal tab, painted in official, state-highway-department-issue reflectorized green, with the dirty white letters *HCL* on it. It's easy enough to decipher if you happen to notice it: "Hill City Limits." We're all so used to crossing the boundary during the course of the day, doing business on both sides of it, leaving and entering the city, that it's tempting to overlook the imaginary line: "Oh, yeah. We live in the country, but we do most of our shopping in the city. . . ."

Mobility, money, casual sophistication—but the boundary is real. The language of the city charter ties the legal definition of the city to a very specific portion of the earth's surface: "The territory contained within the following limits shall be deemed and taken as the city of Hill City: Beginning at the point where the right, or southerly bank of Fishing Creek intersects with the southerly bank of Kings River; thence across the mouth of Fishing Creek up Kings River; thence with a straight line . . ."

111

The city is not an idea or a spirit or even a group of people (each one of whom come and go, inevitably); it is a *place,* marked out by the specific delineation of metes and bounds. It was originally laid out along the riverbank, butting up against the high bluffs. The river's canyon is so deep here that you can see bare cliff faces, exposing the rock that is usually hidden by our mediocre clay soil. The rock is old. It has been so squeezed, buried, heated, exposed, buried and squeezed again that it is almost impossible to sort it into neat categories: "Gray biotite—quartz gneiss, quartz micaschist, and graphitic schist, . . . horn blende gneiss and amphibolite in and apparently younger than the enclosing schists and gneisses." At bottom, this is an ancient place. Because the river's even older than the latest wrinkling of the rock, we have some spectacular upstream views of the mountains and the river's great, deep cut through them, especially in the spring and fall.

The people and the buildings and the streets have long since climbed the bluff overlooking the river and spilled south, where the land is higher and flatter and where a description of the metes and bounds of the city limits no longer refers to nature but to what man has done: ". . . thence with the said southerly side of said turnpike to its intersection with Ware's Road; thence along the westerly side. . . ." In its concluding paragraph on the city limits, the charter goes on to define the purpose of the boundary in the dry, formal cadences of the law: "The inhabitants of the territory comprised within the present limits of the city of Hill City as hereinbefore described . . . shall continue to be one body politic in fact and in name under the style and denomination of the city of Hill City. . . ." There is no citizenship by birth, just the good old American *jus soli,* the law of the soil; if you're there, you're part of it. No matter how mobile and unattached you are, whether you regard yourself as part of a "body politic" or not, you are a citizen, at least legally, for as long as you hang your hat here.

So why should political ambition come to rest within such narrow limits and on such an arbitrarily defined people? Why indeed would anyone in their right mind serve on the city council, especially for any length of time? Isn't public service at war with the usual ways of thinking about success, challenge, maybe even responsibility? You're supposed to rise above parochialism and demonstrate merit by being cosmopolitan: "Did you know F's wife flies to Washington once a week, just to have her hair done?" "Uhh . . . no. Guess he's got the money for it." The prevailing visions of success and worth (The guy has so much money his wife can make an airplane trip just to get her hair done!) have little to do with what is fixed, with what can be known and shared only by those in a particular place, with what is forever tied to that place. We bathe ourselves in words and images of being free and placeless. In the mirror of television advertisements, we see ourselves continuously young and always in motion—moving through airports, traveling on jet aircraft, making long-distance telephone calls. Being "someone" is a matter of movement, speed, images: the dazzling psychological satisfaction of a universally admired self. So why "tie yourself down," especially to a place, when our society revels in its ambition to destroy place?

The oath that every council member takes doesn't answer the question. Instead of unlimited aspiration, it offers the opposite: a meager field of limited action. We are supposed to reach for transcendence, but the oath offers instead duty and the constant, nagging reminder that elevation to official position is always balanced by the limits of the law: "I do solemnly swear that I will support the Constitution of the United States, and the Constitution of the State, and that I will faithfully and impartially discharge and perform all the duties incumbent on me as a member of the city Council of Hill City according to the best of my ability. So help me God."

Duty, law, this office—is this why it's so hard to get people to run for city council? Is it really asking a lot of them to urge them to focus their energies on this fifty square miles, these seventy-thousand people, and to put up with the complexities of office itself? Folkways go against it in several parts of town. In one of his quarterly reviews of life among the country-club set, T. noted that it was well understood that one should "never go anywhere near City Hall—[never] have anything to do with city government." That's an easy enough resolution to keep if you're convinced you can get what you need just by asking, but then don't ask so there's no risk of being socially embarrassed if you turn out to be mistaken.

L. evidently reflects this mind-set held by The Few when she iterates her familiar line: "I don't care about running for office; I prefer to exercise power behind the scenes. . . ." The joke is that she's the model of an ineffective partisan "operative," incapable of anything beyond hanging on to her obscure party post. Claims to "behind the scenes" influence are usually made in personal conversation and may be taken as ritual expressions of egoism, not as serious factual claims. Besides, how durable or useful could such "influence" be if it can't be exercised in public? So even though it's only grudgingly acknowledged in some quarters, those of us who get elected still qualify in most people's minds as being some part of civic leadership, whatever that is. With being elected and getting a real, official title does come recognition, but something else comes as well, something that is not quite the same as recognition but is a little strange and unexpected: access to public attention. For example, private citizens may call press conferences, but only at their own peril. The reporters may or may not show up. But if a member of the city council calls one, they'll show up—eagerly, if there's even a whiff of controversy about it. Having attended, they will devote space or airtime to what was said, respectfully setting out the statements in an "objective" way, putting nonsense on an equal footing with accurate information and giving manipulative propaganda the same status as honest inquiry. Whether some choose to acknowledge it or not, the members of city council, and especially the mayor, have the peculiar quality of serving as symbols for the community.

How we look, how we act, what we say, how we express ourselves, and how we understand ourselves are all reference points that people use as they watch and listen: "Tell C. to stop clearing his throat with the microphone on. It sounds like a jet airplane taking off. Really, it's very distracting." "You ought to lose some weight. Then you could run for higher office." "What did he say that for? That was ugly." "You really oughtta go. People expect you to be there." There's no break at all between these assessments and their creators' expression of what the community *is* to them: "Ah, it's always the same. Council sits up there and makes their own decisions. They don't give a damn what anybody thinks." "I really wish he wouldn't act like this is Mayberry, RFD." "Y'know, the city government is really pretty sophisticated and well run. But don't tell anyone. If they found out, they'd vote you all out of office." "As usual, nothing ever happens around here." "At last there's somethin' goin' on around here. I'm really glad to see it."

Street talk doesn't treat the city in an analytical, quantitative way. When people in Hill City talk about Hill City, they want to combine thinking and doing; they want to communicate something about what they see as the essential qualities of the city and their own reactions to those qualities. Becoming a member of city council means getting thoroughly mixed up in all this. Once elected, you become a point of reference for people as they make their running decisions (or nondecisions) about what the city currently means (or doesn't mean) to them. It's startling to find out that even though you see yourself as the "same person," others see you in a new light. Symbols focus how people feel about things in the way that the flag concentrates how people feel about the United States as a whole. In a similar, though obviously less compelling way, council members represent (in the deep sense of the word—re-present, become the manifestation of the community in another form) Hill City to those who live it. They come to be the focus of what people like about the city, what they don't like about it, what they despair of, what they hope for: "We really appreciate what you've done for Hill City over the years." "Well, I can see you don't care what I say. You're going to do just what you want to do, and I'm sorry I live in your ward." "I don't know how we can talk about trying to keep business . . . then when one guy is down on his luck . . . no one's going to lift a finger. . . ." "Y'know, we really've got a lot going for us. . . . We're an undiscovered jewel."

Sensing this symbolic role is something you find out the first day after the election. Consider this discussion, from one of the fairly regular workshops for city officials that are held around the state. This workshop was in an ordinary motel conference room on the north side of Capital City. The group was made up of fairly predictable-looking, middle-aged men who had been in office for awhile. (One had driven all the way from west of the Ridge in his panel van with his business signs all over it—services, rates, phone number.) After the formal, academically approved program had pretty well run its course, everyone relaxed and opened up about things they were used to keeping quiet. The press wasn't there, and, as near as I could tell, no one had come with a member of an opposing faction from their own jurisdiction. So I asked: "Do you remember what it was like the day after you were elected for the first time?" There was only a moment's pause, then smiles of recognition and knowing nods: "Oh, yeah. Nothing prepares you for that, does it?" "Nothin' like it . . . nothin' at all."

We had all experienced something that we couldn't share with those who hadn't been through the same thing. There's no handbook to tell the newly elected council member how to handle his new position; no cheerful "human relations expert" has developed guidelines for the novice. Only those who have gone through it even know about it. The cumbersome ritual of popular election, directed by the minutely detailed, impersonal requirements of the law (filling out forms, qualifying for the ballot, getting things notarized, making financial reports, and so on) leads not only to the institutional decision that Z. is not just another candidate, but the winning candidate who will hold the statutorily created and defined office, but also that Z. is something else, something that bears no mark of ponderous institutional matters. In getting elected and becoming one of the formally designated leaders of the city, Z. will get another dimension added to his personality. That new dimension is changeable and elusive. It is essentially emotional, but not private. It is an odd, public thing. On top of everything else, Z. becomes a part-time psycho-social lightning rod.

The existence of this new role is one of the great revelations of the actual experience of elected office. It demonstrates something so different from the ways we usually think and speak about politics, and it is still so central to the lived reality of office, that officeholders are required to do two almost contradictory things at the same time: they are prohibited from ever saying anything about it, but nevertheless they have to keep it always in mind. Like the focal mystery of some primitive religion, it cannot be addressed directly. It must be addressed indirectly, and even then more in ritual than in words. It doesn't show itself, but it is nonetheless manifested.

One of the things this new role reveals to the officeholder is the shallowness of the formulas so frequently offered as guides to what we should do in office. The familiar prescriptions just don't hold. For example, take the simple, instrumental view so beloved by populists, that "representatives" are there to do "what the people want them to do." Here is one local rendition of the formula: "It's really very simple. We, the voters, hire these guys. If we hire them, we can fire them when they don't do what we tell them." Yeah. The power to hire and fire—very appealing, especially for those whose thinking is organized around force and causation. The emphasis on "doing" even gives it the tone of a practical argument.

But it's only the sound of practicality, not the substance of it. Maybe at one level it's theoretically true—a government that does what people really don't want done rapidly becomes obnoxious and despised. But surely this is as true for a dictatorship as it is for us, and few people get elected with an agenda full of things that no one wants done. In any event, there are so few decisions clearly defined in advance and so few occasions where public opinion is firmly developed that "what the people want" is rarely clear and detailed. Of the sixty or seventy formal decisions the council makes a month, most never get any publicity at all, much less general public reaction. Besides, as X. says, "issues are made, not born." The acceptance of the understanding that "issues" don't occur naturally or spontaneously, but are generated by someone working at it, is evidenced in conversation: "If that son-of-a-bitch hadn't gone out and stirred this up, we wouldn't have heard a goddamn thing. Now we've got to clean up his shit. . . ." Or, from the opposite perspective, but using the same metaphor: "If there's shit, stir it. The more you stir it, the more it stinks. . . . Sooner or later, something will happen."

More imaginatively, there are the words of a housepainter, talking to me at a private gathering. He was dressed in jacket and tie, the sleeve seam of his jacket coming apart at the shoulder. His tired, pretty wife was standing loyally next to him, evidently worried about the time he was devoting to politics instead of to business. "What you've got to understand," he said, "is 'creative issues.' Here's what I mean: there's a neighborhood where the creek overflows into a lot of backyards every time there's a big rain because of a new development upstream. Maybe they all just think that's the way it's got to be. What you do is go into the neighborhood and start asking questions. Pretty soon the people start talking about it. Then it's an issue—'Why isn't the county doing something?' That's 'creative issues!'" Maybe that's why not many things become issues. Somebody has to work at creating them.

Besides, Hill City residents aren't very fond of issues, though a certain amount of pleasure is taken in occasional public fights. What our residents mostly want is for things to be taken care of without a lot of whoop-de-do or unnecessary expense. They have a way of short-circuiting the alleged necessity of investigating everything and following the tedious back-and-forth between proponents and opponents of whatever is before them. If something's not tangibly messed up, they're satisfied with having a sense of knowing and trusting whoever's making the decisions. Well, maybe "trust" is too enthusiastic a word—it's more like having a residual sense that whatever gets messed up will still cause less inconvenience than having to take time of one's own to straighten things out. So in place of finding out about all the doing, they form summary assessments of the council members' public personalities. For example, a lot of people seem to like to watch the meetings now that they're on cable TV. They like to appraise political style: "He just sits there, and I can't understand him when he does say something. . . ." "I really liked it, knowing he was there. It made me feel good." "You're the only one of the bunch who makes any sense."

Their attention to style is not necessarily frivolous indulgence. Style is an important clue to how a council member will react to novel circumstances or how a member will respond to situations that hadn't been foreseen at election time (which is most of them in these days of two- or three-point platforms). Even though a candidate is "the same person" after they've been elected, they still have to decide what they're going to make of their new public *persona*. Among other things they will have to decide how to respond to different kinds of demands and what they will do if they are to get at least some personal satisfaction from the job. There are those who imagine the life of a public official to be very different from the life of a private citizen. But council members still get bored, still get distracted, and still lose track of what they are doing. It's no matter that they've gotten themselves elected—they still have to live in a particular setting, get through the day, and be able to sleep at night. They still have to decide how to arrange things, what limits they will set to politicking, what they'll turn into an "issue," and what they'll let slide.

More personally, it's necessary to decide what to wear, how to behave, what kind of responses to elicit from the people that are met . . . and to decide when enough is enough. For these personal matters, style is the way of harmonizing the "inner" points of resistance with the "outer" demands of the new, unnerving, governmental environment. For the public, it is as important (maybe even more important) to have an understanding of these things as it is to identify a handful of "positions" that have been taken on whatever matters are currently defined as "issues." The clues to how all of the unforeseen things will be handled are gleaned from the style of a council member in setting about the work of the council.

The importance of being able to deal with the unforeseen is usually appreciated only in the clear vision of hindsight. For all of his meticulous care in training people, in generating high morale, and in planning constantly, C. is modest, almost shy, about what he does as an administrator. But in one unguarded moment he let slip a burst of pride. He had been doing some stock taking and liked the results: "I've been thinking. In the past couple of years we've had our toughest winter—all that snow, the worst flood since the city was founded, and the biggest fire in terms of square-feet destroyed. And you know what difference it made?" "Hunh? Not much, come to think . . ." "Right! We didn't miss a beat. It didn't throw us at all!" "Mmm. Yeah, our disasters weren't disasters! I wonder if anyone will ever recognize it?"

No public comment ever did, and the council only discussed it a little. The preceding years had been tough in budget matters, but with all the restrictions on spending, the training money had never been cut out. Usually, training's the first thing to go, and if any council member had ever said anything it would have been. But everyone tacitly agreed that "doing more with less" required more work on morale building and more chances for the staff to develop expertise. There was no public debate—we just did it that way. As a result, the disasters weren't disasters, and nobody noticed.

Holding public office has an inescapably personal element about it that profoundly affects what happens. The personal part is strong enough to feel almost like ownership. Conversations recognize that sense of ownership: "How in the hell did he get such a grip on that seat? He doesn't deserve it, but it's his 'til he dies." Or again: "Ah, stop worrying. You'll be reelected. That seat's yours as long as you want it." Part of the sense of possession is surely vanity and habit, but an even stronger part of it comes from the consciousness of having to build a unique, personal response to being in the office—*your* response. That's one of the reasons political trivia is so personal, no matter what the level: W. is so lazy that he'll pay attention only when signalled by D.; K. goes to every party in sight, while P. goes to none; G. hits the bottle pretty hard, and so on. None are single-motive automatons—constantly seeking power or wealth or whatever. None are automatic registers of someone else's preferences, not even the ones most ready to cultivate pet interests.

For most of the council, most of the time, this is just proof of what it is presumed everyone already thinks—that there's no need to worry about a lot of textbook niceties. Elections happen to be how you get in office. You are here in town and will be here afterward, and what you want is for people to say that what you did was pretty much OK. If you want your friends to keep on speaking to you, it's best to go with the sense of the community most of the time. By the same token, you can't give away the store by saying "yes" to everyone. It's nice to be regarded afterward as having shown a moderate amount of personal strength. So, you need to be careful, be sure you do what you need to do, and work to make sure that what gets done makes sense and is appealing when your term is over. And rather than waste time debating abstract theories or refuting electoral bombast or talking about what it all "feels like," the ones who are any good just say, "Well, I just wanted to get a few things done."

This last statement is absolutely correct. The only point of being in office is to get something done for the community. It is not a Pollyannaish claim at all: it is the point. That wanting to get something done might not be the only motivation, that more personal motives might enter in, is where commentators and critics get hung up looking for the "real" motive—but the city seems able to tolerate mixed motives. What is done might be tangible—major buildings, public works projects, different programs; it might be something less tangible, but just as real—a better attitude, a willingness that wasn't there before. And, actually getting something done does involve "learning the ropes" of the organization.

Being governmental, everything in city politics is defined by law. For most people, that makes it unattractive to start with, but it is even more unattractive to most because it does not deal with those few parts of the law that seem at least a little familiar—like the Bill of Rights or federal entitlement legislation—but is instead nearly all state legislation, never popularly discussed or detailed in the classroom and rarely in the news media, even though it's presumably "closer" to us. In addition to being a part of fairly obscure state law, the city deals with an obscure corner of it— local-government law: the onerous doling out of offices, powers, and responsibilities; the quibbling state supreme court decisions that parse and qualify what manages to get into the statute books; and on and on. Maybe that's why popular superstition has it that lawyers are the ones best suited to hold office. Having to think first about not running afoul of the dull, merciless commands of the lawbooks, and only afterward doing some-thing, seems to be a heavy task to impose on ordinary mortals.

Difficult or easy, the broad outlines of what's in the law need to be incorporated into what a council member does. It helps both to know Dillon's rule that "any fair, reasonable doubt concerning the existence of power is resolved . . . against the [municipality]," and to have a feel for its implications, that "these general principles . . . are indisputably settled, but difficulty is often experienced in their application." And it's not just the limits and procedures spelled out in the law; there are also quasi-legal patterns of behavior to absorb—*Robert's Rules of Order Newly Revised*, when we actually go by them, the procedural arrangements of the council itself, the even vaguer matter of what's expected in the way of demeanor. This and more has to be not just learned but also digested: chewed up, swallowed, incorporated. Those with the capacity, habit, or taste for office can do the digesting and not be hampered by it. But some have a harder time of it, perpetually taking the risk of either colliding with the law or becoming dependent on the admonitions of the city attorney.

J. came across as one of the latter types. In his private life he was a midlevel, white-collar employee of a very large corporation, but in govern-ment he had regularly upset people by trying to go around procedures. Just as regularly, he would look to the city attorney not just for advice but also for actual direction. N. was far worse, ignoring significant matters of law and using the press to urge actions that were popular and plausible-sound-ing, but legally impossible. C., a lawyer, would push proposals he sup-ported to the legal limit; it was fun to watch, but tough on the city attorney.

But no matter how intriguing (or boring) it is to learn the procedures and become aware of limits, timing, priority, and sequence, they are nothing more than the prerequisites for actually getting down to doing something. And the "something" is out there, outside the comfy interior of City Hall. The procedures are only the means, not the purpose of anything, though it is a great purpose to have law be the means by which we act in harmony with whatever personal style has been adapted. Procedures have to be understood as the way of operating in order to get anything done. However obvious that becomes from the perspective inside City Hall, those outside frequently seem not to recognize it at all. And complaining about how no one outside City Hall understands is common: "Can't they understand that if they really want the project built, then the first thing that has to be done is. . . . Only after that do you . . ." "Ah. They're like everyone else. They think we can just wave a magic wand. . . ." It's hard to explain, especially to people who are excited, but the tedium of carefully prescribed procedure necessarily spreads over all the city government's activities.

Even small matters can create a certain amount of administrative disruption: fix this pothole now (forget the work flow in the Streets and Utilities Division); get out to Forest Acres, Mrs. Q. is pitching a fit about the leaves (divert a truck from a neighborhood where the emotionally less volatile can be prevailed upon to be patient). It's easier when a request can be handled in the ordinary course of things. It's easier yet if the ordinary course of things is clearly organized so that they can be professionally done by people who give a damn about what they do and take pride in it. For example, back when I was first elected, I got an impassioned letter from a resident generally considered to be "outspoken." Happily, it wasn't just another ration of hot air; it contained a reasonable request for changing some street lane markings on Outer Avenue to accommodate a center-of-the-road turn lane. I sent a prompt response, promising to "look into" the matter and asked the city manager what could be done. As it turned out, the traffic people had been wondering whether to do something like that anyway; the lane markings were scheduled to be redone that week, and the equipment was on the way. With this letter, they had the requisite expression of public interest, so they did it immediately. In just a few days I got another letter from the same energetic writer, this one filled with praise for me and my obvious ability "to get things done." In addition, he had a list of several more things to be done with the same efficacy that had been so gloriously demonstrated in the matter of the lane markings. I decided not even to answer the second letter; no sense in giving away trade secrets or letting him think he had unlimited access.

Everyone develops his own way of mediating between government and his constituents: W. was generally quiet, occasionally almost secretive; R. was always open and businesslike; S. tended to be selective, but if he took something up he would pursue it in a fanatically manipulative way; J., diligent and good-hearted, was frequently too quick to sympathize; he regularly generated friction by making requests without stopping to reflect on what all might be involved, though he often did his homework more carefully than the rest of us.

So there are things that can be learned from experience—the critical initial choice of personal style, the laborious acquisition of knowledge of the ways of established government, the consequent meshing of those with constituents seeking something, and many more as well, most of which are never publicized. These are not separable things; they are strands in the fabric of how and what is done. By themselves, they are nothing. They are woven together, in some way or other, by the doings of each council member. Making a judgment on these things is an inescapably qualitative matter; it cannot be done by any simple measure of counting up something and approving the highest score. At the very center of our word-soaked, populist democracy—with all its panoply of free and unfettered speech, investigative journalism, open government, fervent expressionism, and all the rest—lies a hub that is silent. Because of its silence, it is almost secret. It has quite different qualities than those we usually associate with politics. It is more qualitative than quantitative; it is highly personal, not something external. It is not much discussed, so it has no name. For lack of anything else to call it, I will call it "practical character." *Practical* suggests something associated with doing, with tangible matters; *character* suggests something we usually treat as different from practical things, the moral qualities of a person. Combining the two identifies the moral qualities that a person brings to an activity.

The practical character of an officeholder is recognizable to many in office, even if it is not able to be named. It doesn't seem to attract much attention from those outside of office, even those who follow government avidly. I still recall the occasion, at a dinner party, when I began to recognize how deep the difference is between those who grasp the value of practical character and those who ignore it. It was the kind of social event that is held in academic settings, maybe particularly in southern academic settings, and was a welcome break in the routine of a federally funded session for college teachers at the university in Metro City during a hot, steamy July. We were there to study and discuss some of the more esoteric aspects of twentieth-century political theory, and one of our hosts, on find-ing out there were two in the group who actually held office, arranged a din-ner on the theme of theory and practice. It was a thoughtful gesture; the guest list consisted of a handful of activists, professors with interests in po-litical theory, the two of us in the conference who had been elected to public office, and a third officeholder, an older gentleman, evidently a friend of the university, who had been a member of the state legislature years before. He had been a moderate during the divisive battles over racial integration, and he was therefore qualified as a battle-scarred veteran of real political wars.

The dinner was at someone's house, which gave us the feeling of having been sealed off from the world—it was old, still furnished in the style of the 1940s and 1950s. There wasn't much air-conditioning, and the shades were drawn to keep out the heat of the late-afternoon sun.

I can't remember the particulars, but the conversation finally boiled down to the three practitioners against the activists and intellectuals. The practitioners (one feminist Democrat, one neo-Whig Republican, and one traditional Democrat—a broad range of the political/ideological spectrum) ended up arguing together, against the others, in favor of a common theme: the importance of character in determining the desirability of an officeholder. We argued that partisan loyalty and ideological stance aren't as important as personality, which we interpreted in a broad sense as how someone understands their office and acts in it. The others were reluctant to approve of the idea that government policy-making revolved in any significant way around the personalities of those making the policies. One older woman—the wife of the former legislator, I think—got downright annoyed with us. She was an officer in The League of Women Voters, or something like that, at a fairly high level. She was concerned with legisla-tive scorecards, campaign promises, ideological consistency and the like. We had laid down with almost no disagreement what we thought made a good colleague from the perspective of actually trying to make govern-ment work: not his partisanship or ideology or his "magnetic" public presence, those things that occupy so much of the attention of political observers, but things like doing his homework, being discreet and trust-worthy, being clear about what he really wanted, knowing how things worked, not pandering to public opinion, looking for areas of agreement rather than just exploiting disagreement, and remembering that any set of decisions would be followed by still more decisions, all while keeping in mind that the public business does have to go on. . . .

The activist ended by being exasperated with us, and the discussion never got much further than understanding that there was a deep gap between the unexpected sides to the argument. What had we stumbled onto? For each of us officeholders, our personal experiences were not just private possessions; they were also raw material, what researchers might be pleased to call "data," that could become part of some more finished project. But those who turned out to be the other side had no such interest; instead, they were impatient and bemused. For them, something was missing. What was it? Some sense of conceptual completion? Had they been expecting a formulation of either process or purpose that focused and concentrated their private understandings? Did they need assurance that ideology or "the system" (or some mutation of the system) could provide a meaningful grasp of what happens? Evidently, they wanted some explanation that made the personalities of those doing the governing no more than random variations whose effects would be self-negating or epiphenomena of something greater. . . . Or maybe they were hoping for servants whose discretion would never be required. Certainly they hadn't wanted to hear a bunch of talk about politics centering on the essential importance of the individuals actually doing the governing.

But the sense that comes from having to do it is that it matters a lot who those individuals are. It's not the usual stupidity of a person having to fit some prespecified mold, the dress-for-success, wow-I'm-impressed, peacock image so beloved by the hangers-on. It's something that has less to do with casual public opinion and more to do with something much less discussed, a very real, if obscure, ability to see what the position requires. It is an ability to move beyond ego-feeding and pressure tactics to see the possibility of something more, something that both includes and subordinates the narrowly political tugs-of-war and puts them in proper perspective by showing how limited their importance really is. What passes for politics is not the real politics—the real politics is something more elusive.

Choosing what words to use to convey this obscure matter of becoming dimly aware of deeper purposes is difficult. Words are weak anyway, and whatever this obscurity is, it is not an all-defining cosmic pattern for some genius to grasp and convey to the rest of us. It's far closer to being something so dispersed and amorphous that it can't be perceived as a whole. The only thing we can do is get our hands on our own chunk of it and talk about that, hoping that there are others doing the same. But it's not easy. People don't expect us to do that, and we are constantly attuning ourselves to people's expectations. There just aren't many occasions where those of us who might be inclined to talk about it have the chance to.

Still, there was that workshop where the participants became so unusually open and reflective, that meeting in the ordinary meeting room in the no-more-than-respectable motel on the north side of Capital City with what seemed to be a fairly ordinary collection of local officials. It was the best response I could ever remember getting at a training session. The atmosphere stayed relaxed and open, so I went ahead with my part of the program: getting the participants to identify the things that could lead them to not do as good a job as they wanted, that could pressure them into making decisions they'd end up wishing they hadn't made. I used the example of H. He was usually a good person to work with—a good listener but a reluctant believer. Maybe it was his years of police work; whatever the source of it, he would on most occasions listen, nod, and then get another opinion. I liked that skepticism, and it worked well. But there was one sort of appeal that got him every time. If a widow of a retired policeman or fireman would call him in a state of emotional distress, he would charge off on a crusade with no hesitation at all, regardless of how impractical or misplaced the plea might be. When he abandoned his ability to think twice, he became a sitting duck, promoting things that wouldn't fly, weakening his influence over events. Having used a friend as an example, I went on to use myself as a bad example: a sucker for appeals from gentility, particularly in the right kind of setting, made by someone who came across as a bright person who had done his or her homework. Women could be especially ingratiating; men were easier to see as competitors.

The group started chiming in; everyone was aware of times they had been tempted into doing what they later felt was wrong: "When somebody says something's 'progressive.' The word's enough; I'll just go for it." "If anyone ever discovers my weakness for saltwater fishing, they'll be able to get me to give away the store. Just invite me to come along, and then when I'm reeling in a big one, ask for the outrageous. . . . I'd go, 'Yeah! Sure! Anything you want!' " The best one was from the older man from west of the Ridge, the one with the panel truck with his plastic signs all over it: "If someone comes and says, 'You're the only one I'm asking to help on this,' I'll do way more than I should. I'll try to prove I'm superman. . . . And they might not even be telling me the truth!" Proof by contraries: the group liked thinking about how to keep from becoming suckers . . . but on the behalf of what? What did we feel we wanted to be true to? No one tried to give it a name, and I didn't either. Certainly not the "public interest." Whatever that is, it is not something calculable or reducible to the kind of numerical gain that the word *interest* implies, even though it does involve a strong sense of being prudent with money and living within the limits imposed by the real world. It's not something external, anyway. Those who get some glimpse of it and then try to treat it as a natural thing, something there on its own, with its own necessity, never understand it either. Like the "little moron" of the old jokes, they're just looking under the brightest street light.

We might say that it's a human possibility, arguing something like this: because in discussing the negative cases the discussants must implicitly refer to a positive, they have experienced some such positive; this elusive positive is encountered only within the context of governance; but still, it doesn't have to be encountered. Maybe we should leave it at that. It's not an idea or a principle or whatever—it's just a human possibility, period. It's not necessary, it's not inevitable, it's just something that might be, but, again, might not.

But then what is it the possibility *of*? It's not confined to just one factor because it's perceptibly the coming together of a number of things. Perhaps that's the secret of place; only by confining yourself to a place can you become aware of successions and relations, of intertwinings and unravelings. What is done has to somehow be in harmony both with who is giving shape to the doing and the multiple mysteries of the place itself. The only word that comes to mind that suggests such a tying together is the not-so-popular *integrity*. But that is a weak word, too; it suggests something frosty and remote in some stiff way, and it's not that at all. Only if we can use integrity in the sense of "integer"—that which cannot be divided, that which is whole in itself—or maybe "integrate"—combine, meld, make whole—does it start to convey something about the human possibility of bringing things together.

But it is always a matter of some actual, identifiable persons harmonizing the perceptions and projects of a bounded place. What can government be if it is not that? It's hard to imagine. But if government is that, the implications are enormous: responsibility rests first on us. Maybe that was what W. meant when, in the early stages of what turned out to be his disastrous gubernatorial campaign, he remarked to me: "Ten years in local government? That's a long time in the trenches." At the time I thought "long time in the trenches" was a curious turn of phrase, but what if he was right? What if here, where we have to live with what we do, where we see people in the supermarket who will recognize us and ask about things, where we have our phone numbers in the book, where we have to figure out how we will live with the consequences of what we do—what if those are "the trenches," the essential work of governance?

How often have I done this? I gather the papers of the evening's formal, bimonthly session into a neat little stack, tap them a couple times on the tabletop to even them out, and walk down the corridor to the soft illumination of the lobby; turn right, stride over to the inner set of doors, push into the shallow vestibule, press against the panic bar on one of the heavy, brass-framed outer doors, and step out into the night; pause again, either at the top of the five steps or at the bottom, on the sidewalk, to size up what's happened in the outer world while we were making decisions that are most likely not as earth-shaking as we suppose. The tableau changes a little depending on the season of the year and the hour of the meeting. Most of the time, it has gotten dark, there's little traffic in the street, lights are on in some of the offices, and a scattering of cars are parked at the curbs up and down the street. The light poles seem more conspicuous at night. The one in front of our dinky City Hall parking lot especially so, its mercury-vapor lamp throwing garish light on the front part of the lot. The back is made even darker by contrast, almost hidden in the gloom at the bottom of the rocky cliff that rises three stories to the top of the hill. The great, outdoor elevator is turned off, its doors locked; so prominent in the daylight, it's almost invisible at night.

I stop for a moment to note who's in the parking lot and who's still in the building—check the sky for weather and let my body adjust to the outside temperature while I play back the meeting in my mind. Tonight's neighborhood-versus-developer fight ended in a compromise, but not a good one. Did anyone else on the council share my worry that the neighborhood had gotten greedy and stupid and that the developer had been greedy and smart, using the agreement that they grudgingly arrived at to extort concessions from us that we wouldn't have made otherwise? We have to talk to the others, but when? how? A lot depends on P., who seems attentive to this stuff only by fits and starts. The corridor land-use revision went okay—finished at last. It took too long, but who cares now? The whole meeting took too long—I wish D. or B. were still on the council; they caught on to things fast and could move the others along. C. is too preoccupied, but who wouldn't be with what he's got on him now? He's popular enough, but he gives people the idea we're just marking time, and that's not the case at all. And how did the terminal building financing get so screwed up? Can I take care of all this, this . . . crap, in a limited amount of time, and put up with the low-level grief on top of it?

Is all this really important, or am I just playing games with myself? The resentment and stupidity . . . or is it just ignorance? I cross the street and get into the car, slinging the evening's accumulation of papers into the other seat, where, no more than three minutes after I have so neatly stacked them, they turn into a jumbled mess once again. The engine's on; this tub's old, but it cranks over right away. I turn the lights on—damned switch is almost busted—and back out of the parking space, turn right onto the street, then cut across for a quick left down to Main and left again to head home. I think of all that did get settled—not bad, really. And there are more people who try to make this stuff easy than there are those who try to make it hard. Maybe there is something very fragile and valuable at stake in this—maybe it's really true that for the community to do well we have to do well—or, if not us (everyone is, by definition, expendable) whoever holds our places. Maybe this is not just a necessary evil or an unpleasant duty but something that can be good, that can justify all the effort. There's no choice anyway. I'll stick it out for a little while longer. Up the hill and through the inner-city commercial district—aging brick buildings and peeling storefronts—then out to where the commercial buildings are fewer and the houses farther apart. Things are very quiet this time of night. I'll get a good night's sleep—things will look better in the morning.

Epilogue

Acting concerns action, doing concerns the deed,
loving the beloved, joy the object of joy.
—Edmund Husserl, *Ideas*

Governing is not a concept or an embodiment of principles; it's not even a fulfillment of history or the crystallization of some preexisting "will of the people." Governing is a real, live, human activity, singular each time it is brought about. At the same time it shares all the traits of everything else we do—it drains effort, uses up time, is prone to error, and occasionally rises above the petty and obvious. Paradoxically, it is like human activity in general and also possesses an identity that belongs to it and to nothing else. Above all, it doesn't just happen; it does not come automatically, as a "result" of "factors." It takes place. It is always located in a concrete here and now. It is something done by particular people who may be suited for the responsibility or who may not, who may accomplish something or may merely settle for the appearance of activity. Who these people are individually is not a matter of mere detail. It is the central fact of governance. What they do is not experienced as the "output" of a "system." For the sprawling, complicated set of arrangements we so glibly refer to as "our system" to work, identifiable people have to be there to make it work. Even more people are needed, close at hand, who understand it enough to comment on it, to talk about it, and to keep it a part of public life. We require public discussion of governance in terms of what real, live people do in the here and now.

The sweaty, cramped circumstances of Hill City is the here and now of the narrative above. Hill City is a particular, clearly defined place where anyone who cares to can walk around most of what is done, poke at it, and, above all, talk about it: "Do you think they oughtta be doing that?" "I dunno . . . what do you think?" The citizens of Hill City talk about things that go on because they can be a little skeptical in practical matters (a healthy trait), and they don't like to buy pigs in pokes. So they would rather talk things over first, wait to hear what other people say about them, maybe consider how conspicuous figures react. Only after mulling a matter over do they come to a conclusion, and even then they may not stick with it. They reserve the right to change their minds if they don't like the results, and they can even ignore a matter entirely if they don't think it's worth the bother. For us in office, there isn't much point in trying to reduce what we do simply to following public opinion, and anyone who tries to do it ends up tying himself in knots. Public opinion has its own integrity. In the constant background of talk, of the chatter of the marketplace, the chorus chooses its own direction even as it watches the posturing of the principal actors. Public opinion will not allow itself to be used to justify something that turned out poorly, unless it is self-deceived.

Some people still seem to recognize that the governing we do is not reducible to something else. Like all human activity, it has a final mystery about it. It reveals itself incompletely, always half-veiled by the context of daily life. It is grasped as much by inference and interpretation as by the tedious river of words that we set down on paper month after month. Clearly, for our little place there is no "history," just a mosaic of memories, some vivid and some fading. If those of us who temporarily hold the official positions of Hill City's governance actually accomplish anything, it is by somehow knitting together the intertwined complexities of the particular things that officials do so that it makes some kind of sense to those who live here. If there is any power in this, it is a power that is not clear and mechanical; it is not a power where force is applied at one end of a mechanism and a predictable result pops out at the other end. If this power is like anything at all, maybe it is more like natural electricity, sometimes controllable and sometimes not. Maybe it is even like the wind, perceptible only in the traces it leaves behind.

What is done with this quasi-natural force—whether it is channeled or allowed to disperse, whether it is well directed or mistakenly led astray, whether there is a reasonable public understanding of those who presume to do the directing or not—is a matter on which there is a curious, disquieting silence. Somehow, the very real intelligence that the people of Hill City have when they take the time to seriously consider practical and tangible things weakens and dissipates. Bombast and nonsense can take over; discussion stops. All too often, the theater of politics is taken for politics itself, and everyone becomes an expert on what is presented on the nightly news. They become definitive arbiters of whether this tone of voice, that gesture, was "convincing" or not. Appearance enjoys another little victory over reality. The populist delusion, "every man a king," slips into, "every man a patron of the arts," then slides down into something like, "every man an authoritative critic."

Worst of all, those at the state and federal levels of government seem willing enough to buy into this disembodied sense of citizenship: just get an impression, then make an indisputable judgment. Period. In this feeble view, the definitive act of citizenship is not to care for the community in some way; it is merely to express a preference in the voting booth—that's enough.

The representatives we elect to Congress and the General Assembly seem content to accept the role this assigns to each of them by going off to a set of famous buildings, becoming part of a "process," and then staying alive politically on personal constituent work, name recognition, and smiles in the right places on "visits to the district." Only from time to time do they exercise their authority; mostly they are content to tinker with this single item or fiddle with that one, or develop programs and policies that they can claim to direct but that are in fact carried out mostly by local government. Most often, they take the usual approach to those of us that hold office at this parochial level: "Do just this much. . . . We won't tell you how to take care of the rest. You take care of the nuts and bolts."

So much for the possibility that wisdom is lodged with higher authority. Nuts and bolts. The old, worn formula that everyone agrees with, whether it's true or not, whether we believe it or not. Despite what is said, we know that it is no such thing at all—more like nerves and guts, the stress and fatigue of trying to knit together what so many can tear apart so easily.

A handful of very fallible people must assume responsibility for what makes our fragile city a city. What we know and cannot say is that the actual process of governing can draw these people out of themselves, if they really attend to their jobs. They can be drawn into something broader and more vivid than private life, something that is at the same time elevating but also more exasperating, something that leaves them more exposed and vulnerable. Very rarely, governing provides an occasion for the coming together of thousands of impulses into a brief common understanding. More often, all that is possible is to encourage a little decency in a world that doesn't have much time for it. Often, our government is taken for granted, even despised, but the very same critics will turn around and frantically seek it when they think they have need of it. Contrary to all the talk about the "will of the sovereign," our governing is always tentative and provisional.

The loud, confident wordmongers would have us think something quite different. They would have us believe that before government does anything, there will be a recognizable debate somewhere first, that some relevant collection of people will agree on substantive matters, that their supposed agreements can be reduced to words that accurately reflect the agreement, that those words can be translated into an action that is conformable to the now-remote original agreement, and that someone will actually pay attention through this whole train of improbable connections. For those naive or blind enough to imagine that something like this could actually hang together in a world where people lie, get confused, and quit work early, the glorious final conclusion is that the particulars can be depended upon to take care of themselves. After all (said in a tone of voice trying to convey finality, to turn an indefensible prejudice into a brute, unquestioned "fact"), they're just the nuts and bolts. Which, of course, they aren't. There are no nuts and bolts at all; there are only people and what they do. There's no "machinery," either—no "system" of sure operation and guaranteed results. There are only the accumulated expectations and habits and ways of doing that may be permanent, but are just as likely to be on the verge of dissolution. There is no handbook, no step-by-step procedure for achieving a predictable outcome. There is just what we do as we set about our small part in governing, doing reasonably well or maybe not. There is not even "the people," just people we encounter between birth and death, both attentive and absorbed in other things, capable by fits and starts and also given to daydreams and fecklessness.

But that's not bad, or even regrettable. Maybe something can be held together, kept whole, at least for a while. After all, we don't have to concentrate on the nonsense. No one pays attention to it for long, anyway. The life of the city itself provides the coherence, the life of the city that we live in while we try to govern it. If we listen, it will speak, though in a muted and indirect way, constantly murmuring and shifting, offering reminders and little lessons about what is trivial and not worthy of attention, about what is finally true.

Most finally of all, so the astronomers tell us, nothing will last. The earth itself, the seemingly eternal granite on which the city rests, is doomed to become frozen dust, spinning through space in perpetual orbits around a collapsed and lifeless sun. With more relevance, the city's monuments remind us that each of us ego-centered bipeds will die. No hero, no figure great or insignificant has escaped. No "history," no "destiny," no "manifestation of the spirit of the age" can change any of this.

But this is not news. This is only what we already knew, something that would hardly bear repeating if we were not so drunk on ideas and burdened with words. It is so simple that it is comforting; if we are granted here no more than we are able to do, then we are indeed able to do something with what we have been granted, something of value to this place and this people, to the city that is before us. It is quite enough if we somehow foster the growth of both civility and honest achievement. If somehow we can refill the reservoir of decency, if we can contrive for a season to protect innocence and goodwill, it will have been worthwhile.

A Personal Bibliography

This work is a first-person account. It is not drawn from any other source or constructed according to any accepted pattern, but I do hope it can make a contribution to the study of politics. In both style and substance, the manuscript grew out of an informing context that is very concerned with how politics is studied; this context requires acknowledgment. This essay proposes, then, not to review the literature in a recognized subfield, but to indicate some works of scholars and authors that I have used over a period of time to explore the possibility that the direct experience of political activity is an irreducible part of empirical political study. Of course, the authors cited are not responsible for whether I understood them properly or made correct use of their works. They and their heirs need only take whatever measure of satisfaction there is in noting that I found them illuminating in understanding practical matters, and that I recommend them to others.

Most people write about government in one or the other of two ways. Those who have been in government construct memoirs that tell what "really happened." Those with some claim to an external way of knowing offer "objective" accounts of governmental reality. Neither model proved useful when I tried to write about the experience of being an elected official; both felt strained and artificial as I struggled for a way to express for a critical audience the empirical data of the direct experience of holding elective office.

"Back to the things themselves," Edmund Husserl's famous dictum, proved to be the guide for my own effort and also the source of some clues about why the two models seemed so inadequate. The first model is based on unwarranted confidence in what Husserl calls the "natural standpoint"— the unquestioned assumption that what presents itself to our senses is the "real" world. Of course, it's not quite that way. You and I may live on the same planet, but, in the seventeenth-century words of Jeremy Taylor, the world is "like a dove's neck or a changeable taffeta, that looks otherwise to you who do not stand in the same light as I do." What we perceive is profoundly structured by our perspective and our presuppositions. Though Husserl's *Ideas* (W. R. Boyce Gibbon, trans. New York: Collier Books, 1931; reprint, 1962) is difficult and subject to some controversy, I take as unimpeachable his argument against the ability of anyone to grasp the "real" world directly. Thus, an autobiographer who does not take his own perceptions into account sacrifices the possibility that what is written may illumine concerns other than his personal ones.

In his most accessible work, *The Crisis of European Man* (Quentin Lauer, trans. New York: Harper and Row, 1934; reprint, 1965), Husserl shaped his critique of "objective" knowing around the observation that external analyses of social events cannot, on their own terms, give any account of the meaning that the events have for the participants. If one of the purposes of science is to eventually secure the application of general laws or probabilities to practice, the exclusion of meaning from science substantially weakens any claim that the findings of science (understood in these terms) can actually be applied to human experience. The significance of Husserl and other writers associated with phenomenology for political theory is authoritatively treated in the works of Fred R. Dallmyer, such as *Beyond Dogma and Despair* (Notre Dame: University of Notre Dame Press, 1981) and *Critical Encounters* (Notre Dame: University of Notre Dame Press, 1987).

Some years ago, my awareness of the personal character of knowledge was sharpened by Michael Polanyi's *Personal Knowledge* (New York: Harper and Row, 1958; reprint, 1964) in a lasting way. At about the same time, I encountered Eric Voegelin's *The New Science of Politics* (Chicago: University of Chicago Press, 1952) and his convincing argument that how a community represents itself in symbols and thus expresses its meaning to its own members should be a central question in the study of politics. In his *Order and History* (5 vols. Baton Rouge: Louisiana State University Press, 1956–1987), Voegelin applies much of this argument to larger civilizations. Distinguished scholars have explicated Voegelin's work; I have consulted the writing of William Havard and Dante Germino, for example, with profit.

In the matter of methodology, I subscribe to Paul Feyerabend's position as presented in *Against Methodology* (New York: Schocken, 1978). His notion—that methodology should be viewed in the spirit of play—is not frivolous or destructive; it is intensely practical. This should not be construed as an effort on my part to take the side of literature against mathematics in the study of politics. For anyone who proposes to engage in governance, there is an absolute necessity for at least a sketchy literacy in the grimmest branches of number-crunching—accounting and auditing. The number of legislators who fantasize that they can offer any overall control of a budget without such an ability is quite large and should be regarded as a national scandal and an explanation of why our public finance is in such disorder. The same can be said for such policy-making statistical tools as "risk assessment." But in the lived world of governance, there is also a need to have ways of knowing purely qualitative things, such as how to tell the difference between someone who is angrily defensive about a particular matter and someone who is looking for a political fight. The test of a methodology is what we find out, not something within the method itself.

What we want to find out grows, in turn, out of what we encounter. The works of Alfred Schutz, such as *The Phenomenology of the Social World* (Evanston: Northwestern University Press, 1932; reprint, 1967) and his *Collected Papers* (3 vols. Netherlands: Martinus Nijhof, 1962–1966), explicate the understanding of society as encounter with other people. The reminder that society is other people brings to mind Martin Buber's ethics of "I-Thou" relationships, but politics is encounter with others in terms of something else—the power of the state and how it is used. The concept of triadic dialogue, encounter with others in relation to a mutual project, is admirably developed in John Scudder and Algis Mickunas, *Meaning, Dialogue, and Enculturation: Phenomenological Philosophy of Education* (Lanham, Md.: Center for Advanced Research in Phenomenology, University Press of America, 1985).

Additionally, it should be noted that what we encounter is not confined to other people: we live in a physical and embodied world, and politics involves this as well. Charles Goodsell's *The Social Meaning of Civic Space* (Lawrence: University of Kansas Press, 1988) is an architectural survey of a number of American city-council chambers and a shrewd interpretation of the impact of their design on those who act in them. An intriguing study of acting in public is contained in Richard Sennett's *The Fall of Public Man* (New York: Random House, 1974). The embodied character of social existence is one of the major teachings of Maurice Merleau-Ponty in *The Phenomenology of Perception* (Colin Smith, trans. London: Routledge and Kegan Paul, 1962).

Perhaps these approaches, broadly put, can be lumped under the increasingly familiar rubric of "interpretation." Whether or not that is an accurate characterization, I found much of value in Hans-Georg Gadamer's

Reason in the Age of Science (Frederick G. Lawrence, trans. Cambridge: MIT Press, 1981). And I own a well-used copy of Clifford Geertz's collection of essays, *Local Knowledge* (New York: Basic Books, 1983). Interpretation is more commonly used in the investigation of literature, where what would require elaborate and extended discourse in social science can be rendered as character and setting. According to Paul Ricoeur, a "well-chosen example" can illuminate a broad phenomenon ("Phenomenology and the Social Sciences," *The Annals of Phenomenological Sociology* 2 [1977]: 145–60). "Well-chosen examples" are not quite the same thing as "war stories." Offering narrative accounts of singular events for interpretation is not a free-form activity; it has disciplinary requirements, as Donald Polkinghorne points out in *Narrative Knowing and the Human Sciences* (Albany: State University of New York Press, 1988).

It may be worth noting that both novels cited in the chapter headnotes can be said, from the political perspective, to be descriptions in terms of daily life of the consequences of power ignorantly and forcefully used.

The moral importance of daily life is a lesson I idiosyncratically draw from Plato's *Republic* and Aristotle's *The Politics*. Since both of these writers are associated with the birth of rational discourse in politics, perhaps they are appropriate reference points on which to close. It is significant that Socrates' depiction of his ideal state begins at a dinner party and among friends who have just attended a civic celebration. The question of justice and how to pursue it arises as the topic of a free and open conversation. There is an earthy and practical element in the classics, perhaps more obviously present in writers like Hesiod or figures like Diogenes. And if, as even the idealistic Plato puts it in Books VIII and IX, lasting achievement of the ideal is impossible, then there is something to be said for Aristotle's argument that we can foster happiness by working to have the best practical city.